RELISH
CUMBRIA
THE LAKE DISTRICT

Original recipes from the region's finest chefs

First Published 2010
By Relish Publications
Shield Green Farm, Tritlington,
Northumberland NE61 3DX

ISBN 978-0-9564205-1-0

Publisher: Duncan L Peters
Design: George Hole, room501 publishing
Editorial Proofing: Emma Riley
Photography: NR Photography & KG Photography
Printed By: Balto Print Ltd, Stratford,
London E15 2TF

RELISH
PUBLICATIONS.CO.UK
www.relishpublications.co.uk

004
CONTENTS

DESERTS

RESTAURANTS

INTRODUCTION WITH NIGEL MENDHAM

As a chef there isn't a better place to live and work than in Cumbria. Before I moved up to this unique region it was synonymous with two characteristics in my mind – fantastic local produce and breathtaking scenery. This isn't a coincidence. The fresh Lakeland air, diversity of soil and purity of water make this region truly special for the most discerning foodies.

It isn't just the quality that stands out for me now it's the sheer wealth and uniqueness of produce available on your doorstep. Every nuance in Cumbria's landscape is utilised to create a huge variety of produce. Take Scarfell Pike the highest place in England and a pretty inhospitable place for livestock you may think. Well a favourite of mine and one of the recipes in the book is Herdwick Mutton and these sheep can be found in and around the Scarfell area. In Cumbria, the coast and the sea often tend to be overshadowed by the lakes and mountains of the inland areas but this stretch of the Irish Sea contains some fantastic marine life including lobsters and langoustines.

The county also has a lot to shout about when it comes to its culinary creations. Two good examples of this are the Cumberland Sausage and Sticky Toffee Pudding. The original recipe for sticky toffee pudding was conceived at the Michelin starred Sharrow Bay hotel, recipes from the hotel can be found later on in this cookbook. The infamous Cumbrian sausage was borne through the spice trade links between Cumbria and the West Indies in the 16th and 17th Centuries. These links are often the reason that 'traditional' Cumbrian dishes have a hint of quirkiness.

From Michelin starred restaurants to gastro pubs and cafes, Cumbria offers the best in food and drink, day or night. The abundance of superb local produce is combined with individual creativity to provide for even the most discerning foodies.

Nigel Mendham
Described by The Times as 'a master of local produce' Nigel Mendham is the newest Michelin starred chef in Cumbria. Nigel is the Head Chef at The Samling hotel near Ambleside – see page 148 for more details.

8
BORROWDALE GATES HOTEL

Grange in Borrowdale, Keswick, Cumbria CA12 5UQ

01768 777 204
www.borrowdale-gates.com

Welcome to Borrowdale Gates, one of the most beautifully located hotels in the English Lake District.

Our country house hotel is the best-kept secret in the Borrowdale Valley, with log fires, wonderful Lakeland-inspired cooking, and warm, comfortable bedrooms updated in classic modern style – a real home-from-home, on the edge of the hamlet of Grange.

Surrounded by first-class fellwalking country and set in two acres of peaceful, wooded grounds, our Victorian country house is close to the shores of Derwentwater, with the many attractions of Keswick nearby.

This Lake District country house hotel has been lovingly refurbished and updated, blending modern comfort with homely charm and traditional craftsmanship. Built 150 years ago by Margaret Heathcote, benefactress of Grange, every window is a picture frame for the beauty of the Borrowdale Valley. Our dining room looks onto a breathtaking panorama of green pastures where Herdwick sheep graze, up to the slopes of Castle Crag, High Spy, Grange Fell and distant Glaramara. It's a wonderful place to linger over dinner, before curling up with a brandy beside the log fire.

Our head chef, Christopher Standhaven has brought Michelin star experience to the hotel giving the food a modern feel with a French twist, using local produce. The cosy bar and beamed lounge with its wood-burning stove look onto our gardens and the valley beyond. Each bedroom has picture-perfect views to wake up to, whether dusted by wintry frost or glowing with sunshine. Catbells, home of Beatrix Potter's Mrs Tiggy-Winkle, is our magnificent backdrop.

This Lake District country house hotel has been lovingly refurbished and updated, blending modern comfort with homely charm and traditional craftsmanship

PIGEON BALLOTINE WRAPPED IN CUMBRIAN AIR DRIED HAM CHICORY AND PEAR SALAD AND APRICOT CHUTNEY

SERVES 4

Ingredients

Pigeon Ballotine

4 pigeon breasts
1 chicken breast
1 egg white
200ml double cream
4 slices Cumbrian air dried ham
50g dried apricots
50g shallots
5g chopped chives
5g chopped chervil
1 garlic clove
100g thinly sliced Savoy cabbage

Dressing

50ml Chardonnay vinegar
50ml Chardonnay wine
50ml olive oil
50ml vegetable oil

Apricot Chutney

100g dried apricots
1 chopped shallot
10ml wine vinegar
75g brown sugar
pinch of cinnamon five spice

Garnish

20 leaves of red chicory endive
100g wild mushrooms
1 pear
50g hazelnuts
micro herbs

Method

For the Ballotine

Seal off pigeon, set aside.

For the mousse

Blend chicken with salt and pepper, add egg white slowly then add the double cream, place in a bowl and add the apricots, shallots, chives, chervil, garlic and blanched Savoy cabbage. Lay out on cling film the Cumbrian ham, place half the mousse in the middle, lay pigeons on top then mousse on top of that. Roll in roulade shape, tie each end with string to keep in tight and waterproof. Cook in simmering water for 10 -12 minutes and then turn off water and leave for 15 minutes to cool down then place in refrigerator to set.

For the dressing

Reduce by half the vinegar and wine, cool down, add oils slowly and season add pinch of salt and pepper.

For the chutney

Place all ingredients together in a pan, keep cooking and reducing for about 1½ hours slowly until reducing cook out and thick, then place in refrigerator to set.

For the garnish

Pick the chicory into strips, sauté off the wild mushrooms, slice the pear thinly and roast the hazelnuts.

To serve

Slice 4 of the pigeon breasts (remove the cling film after slicing) place together down the plate about ½" apart. Arrange the red chicory, pear and wild mushrooms nicely down the other side of the plate. Sprinkle the hazelnuts and micro herbs place a quenelle of apricot chutney and drizzle the dressing over the chicory leaves, and glaze the pigeon with hazelnut oil.

ASSIETTE OF SHELLFISH, CRAB AND LOBSTER RAVIOLI ROASTED SCALLOP AND A TEMPURA OF LANGOUSTINE

SERVES 4

Ingredients

Ravioli

pasta
250g strong 00 pasta flour
4 eggs
1 yolk
1tbls olive oil
1tbls water
1tsp saffron powder (for colour)

Mousse

1 lobster
200g salmon
200ml double cream
1 egg white
10g chervil

4 scallops

4 langoustine

1 of each carrots, leeks and courgettes

Tempura Batter

1 medium egg
225ml Ice cold sparkling water
100g plain flour
pinch of bicarbonate of soda

Vegetables

baby spinach
tartar mash
capers, gherkins, parsley, shallots
asparagus
broad beans

Method

For the ravioli

First make the pasta; in a mixer add the flour, then mix together the olive oil, water, saffron and eggs, whisk together. When everything is mixed start applying the liquid slowly to the flour until it comes together then knead together by hand for about 3-5 minutes until smooth, leave to rest in refrigerator.

For the mousse

Cook off the lobster in salted boiling water for 7 minutes, refresh and take the meat from the shell.

Take the salmon, blitz and then add egg white, cream until smooth, then take out into bowl and mix in the crab (dry) and lobster (not claws save these for the garnish) chop roughly.

Roll out pasta using a pasta machine and make your ravioli, cut out and refrigerate.

For the scallops

Take out of shell, (you can buy these from your local fishmongers de-shelled).

Roast off scallops until golden brown in colour, de-glaze with lemon butter.

For the langoustine

Blanch in water for 25-30 seconds, just so you can peel them, then lay out some cling film. Julienne the carrots, leek and courgettes, mix well together wrap up the langoustine in the vegetables and then the cling film so the vegetables stick to the langoustine.

For the tempura batter

Place flour and bicarb into a mixing bowl, add egg and whisk then add water, don't mix for too long, works better just mixing so it comes together.

To serve

Cook the ravioli in water for 5 minutes, simmering not boiling so not to spoil the mousse.

Unwrap the langoustine carefully so the vegetables don't come away, then dip in flour, shake them in the tempura batter and deep fry at 170ºC for about 5 minutes, until golden brown, the vegetables will shoot out as the picture.

When all nicely cooked assemble on a plate and serve with fresh baby spinach, asparagus and fresh broad beans.

BABY PINEAPPLE TART TATIN WITH STAR ANISE ICE CREAM AND PINEAPPLE SMOOTHIE

SERVES 4

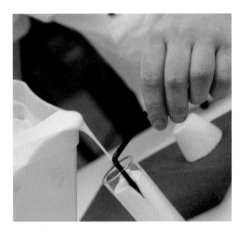

Ingredients

4 baby pineapples
puff pastry square

For Caramel Tins

300g sugar
180g butter

Cardamom Panna Cotta

125ml milk
125ml double cream
3 cardamom pods (crushed)
40g sugar
1 vanilla pod
1 gelatine leaf

Star Anise Ice Cream

200ml milk
300ml double cream
200g sugar
150ml water and 9 egg yolks
3 star anise (crushed)

Pineapple Smoothie

200ml pineapple purée/juice
100ml double cream
squeeze of lemon and lime
50ml sugar

Method

For the tart

First peel and core the pineapple and set aside. Place the sugar and butter in a pan and make caramel, when all mixed together and golden in colour pour into four individual cake tins. When cold it will set (like toffee).

Then roll out your puff pastry (not too thin) and cut into rounds about 6-7 inches. When you have everything ready place the pineapple on top of the caramel and then place the puff pastry on top of the pineapple and leave to rest for 10 minutes.

For the Panna Cotta

Mix all ingredients together except the gelatine leaf and bring to boil. Soak the gelatine leaf in cold water then squeeze excess water out and add to mixture then strain off. Start cooling down over ice until it starts to get thick, then transfer into 4 individual moulds and place in refrigerator to set completely.

For the ice cream

Bring the milk, cream and water to the boil with the crushed star anise. Leave for 2 hours to infuse, then whisk together the egg yolks and sugar for about 10 minutes or until pale yellow.

Bring the milk mixture back to the boil and slowly add it to the egg yolks and sugar whisking all the time, so it doesn't curdle. Place everything back into the pan and cook for a further 10 minutes or until double in thickness, then cool over ice pass off and churn in an ice cream maker. If you don't have one don't worry, place in freezer, it will freeze but not as soft and creamy.

For the smoothie

In a food processor add the pineapple juice lemon and lime. Semi whip the double cream and add the sugar, add the cream mixture to the juice while it's still mixing, mix for about 3-5 minutes and it's ready to pour in your glasses.

To serve

Now place your pineapple tarts in the oven at 180 degrees Celsius for about 15-20 minutes. When the pastry is golden brown take out.

While they are in the oven turn out your panna cottas onto a plate with your pineapple smoothie in a tall shot glass with a straw and a scoop of the ice cream. Then turn out the pineapple onto a tray so it's the right way up so now you should be able to see the nice glazed pineapple. Place onto plate and spoon some of the fruit juices around. Garnish with fresh mint and icing sugar.

18
THE BROWN HORSE INN

Winster, Cumbria LA23 3NR

01539 443 443
www.thebrownhorseinn.co.uk

The Brown Horse Inn is a traditional Lakeland inn set amidst the scenic splendour of the Winster valley. The inn has been owned by Stephen and Karen Edmondson since 2006 and they have transformed it into an award winning establishment.

The Brown Horse Inn strives to provide traditional country fayre using local produce. The majority of its fruit, vegetables and salad is grown in its own nurseries. We don't stop there, a lot of the menu is set around their own meat produce from the Brown Horse estate, which has an array of animals which provides the kitchen team, headed by chef Paul Webster. This includes, pork, lamb, beef, pheasant (from their own shoot days), quail, guinea fowl, goose, duck, venison and turkey.

Not only can you enjoy our traditional home grown and cooked food you can wash it all down with a pint of our own brewed ale. The Brown Horse Inn has recently installed a micro brewery, to which you can enjoy two different ales, one being Old School and the other a Best Bitter.

While indulging yourself at the Brown Horse Inn, why not make a night of it? Currently offering nine newly refurbished en-suite bedrooms within the Inn itself we also have two beautiful cottages within Winster, which are available for letting.

We hope you enjoy our recipes.

While indulging yourself at the Brown Horse Inn, why not make a night of it. Currently offering 9 newly refurbished en-suite bedrooms within the inn itself and also new for 2010, they have 2 beautiful cottages within Winster, which are available for letting

ROAST SEA BASS, CAULIFLOWER PURÉE WITH QUEEN SCALLOPS AND CURRIED CAULIFLOWER BEIGNETS

SERVES 4

Ingredients

4x 120g wild sea bass fillets
28 queen scallops removed from shells and cleaned

Cauliflower Purée

half a trimmed cauliflower
milk to cover
25g of butter
salt
freshly ground white pepper
juice of half of lemon

Curried Cauliflower beignets

half a cauliflower
pinch of chilli powder
pinch of turmeric
pinch of cumin
pinch of coriander
pinch of sugar
pinch of salt
100ml of olive oil

Tempura Batter

¼ of cup cornflower
¾ of a teaspoon of baking soda
pinch of salt
ice cold sparkling water

Basil Oil

40g of fresh basil, stalks removed
100ml of extra virgin olive oil

Method

For the purée

Sweat the cauliflower in the butter with no colour for 8 to 10 minutes then cover with the milk and cook until tender. Then strain keeping the milk, place the cauliflower in a liquidiser.

Squeeze lemon on top, season and blitz adding a few drops of milk until the cauliflower is of a purée consistency.

For the beignets

Cut the cauliflower into small florets, blanch in boiling salted water for 1 min then place into iced water.

Place all the above spices, sugar and salt in a saucepan and warm with the oil to infuse.

Add the cauliflower and marinate for 12 hours. This can be done in advance.

For the tempura batter

Place all dry ingredients in a bowl and whisk in ice cold sparkling water to a batter consistency

For the basil oil

Blanch the basil for 25 seconds in boiling water.

Drain well and liquidise with olive oil.

To cook and dress

Deep fry the beignets in hot oil until golden, drain and keep warm.

Pan fry the sea bass over a medium heat in olive oil, season the fish. Turn when golden; remove from heat to finish cooking through.

Roast the scallops in a hot pan for 30 seconds each side.

To serve

In the middle of a plate, place some of the cauliflower purée.

WINSTER ROE DEER TWO WAYS

SERVES 4

Ingredients

4 x 120g roe deer daubes
4 x 170g roe deer loins
1 carrot
1 shallot
1 stick of celery
1 clove of garlic
¾ of a pint of red wine
10 juniper berries
a little olive oil
1 pint of chicken stock
25g of butter

Chocolate Oil

120g of bitter chocolate
4 tspns of cocoa powder
4 tspns olive oil
80ml of corn oil

Celeriac Purée

½ of celeriac diced
¼ pint of milk
¼ pint of water
pinch of salt
pinch of pepper

Savoy Cabbage

1 savoy cabbage, green leaves only

Confit Root Vegetables

1 large swede
2 large carrots
400g of unsalted butter clarified
2 cloves of garlic
1 sprig of rosemary

Pomme Fondant

4 medium potatoes
pinch of chicken boullion
100g of unsalted butter
pinch of salt
pinch of pepper

Method

For the deer

Place the roe deer in a pan and lightly brown in a little oil

Add the shallot, carrot, celery and garlic, lightly colour and deglaze with the red wine.

Reduce by half, add the juniper and stock, cook on a low heat until very tender. Reduce the liquor to a nice sauce consistency, and keep warm.

For the chocolate oil

Place all the ingredients in to a bowl then place bowl over hot but not boiling water to dissolve.

For the purée

Cover the celeriac with milk and water, cook until tender. Drain, keeping the cooking liqueur then liquidise adding a little of the liqueur to purée. Season and keep warm.

For the cabbage

Blanch for 1 min in boiling salted water and drain, add a little butter and keep warm.

For the confit

Dice the carrot and swede into ½ inch cubes

Cover with the butter and add the rosemary and garlic cook on a medium heat until tender

Drain and keep warm.

For the fondant

Cut the potatoes with a round cutter place on top of butter in a non stick frying pan with the other ingredients.

Cover ¾ of the way with water, cook until tender.

To serve

See photograph.

APPLE PAIN PERDU WITH VANILLA ICE CREAM

SERVES 4

Ingredients

To make the Ice Cream and Custard Base

Please note only use half the mixture for the ice
cream and half for the custard

12 egg yolks
500ml double cream
500ml single cream
350g caster sugar
4 vanilla pods

The Brioche

12g of yeast
30g caster sugar
6g salt
175g softened unsalted butter
1 tbsp of water
300g plain flour
3½ eggs

Apples

4 Coxs Pippin's apples
120g unsalted butter
120g caster sugar
2 tbsp of Calvados

Method

For the ice cream

Place the cream and milk in a pan, split and scrape the vanilla
pods, heat to infuse, now add onto the egg yolks and sugar,
cook over a low heat, to form a custard, without boiling.
Pass and churn.

For the brioche

Mix the yeast and the water together, add a pinch of the sugar
and leave to dissolve. Place flour into a mixing bowl, add the
remaining sugar, salt and yeast mixture, then add the eggs. Add
butter gradually, beat until the mixture slides away from the
bowl. Place in a clean bowl, cover and leave to prove.

When proved place in a baking tin, prove again. Then bake for
30 minutes at 190°C.

For the apples

Peel, core and thinly slice the apples. Melt the butter, sugar and
Calvados in a saucepan. Arrange the apples on a non stick baking
tray in a neat circle. Brush with the butter and sugar mixture,
bake for 7 minutes at 190°C. Take out of the oven, brush again
and put back in the oven for a further 7 minutes until golden,
and keep warm.

Cut out neat rounds of the brioche.

Soak for 1 minute each side in the remaining custard.

In a non stick frying pan add 28g of unsalted butter and colour
the brioche on each side.

To serve

Place on a plate, top with the apples and serve with the
ice cream.

28 CRAGWOOD COUNTRY HOUSE HOTEL

Ecclerigg Windermere Cumbria LA23 1LQ

01539 488 177
www.cragwoodhotel.co.uk

Cragwood built in 1910 for Lancashire industrialist "Albert Warburton" is set in 20 acres of Thomas Mawson garden and woodlands on the shores of Lake Windermere.

Mrs Warburton was widowed in 1935 but was still in residence till after the war, the house being used for evacuees from London.

From 1962 to 1974 a private house for Mr Norman and Mrs Betty Buckley, Mr Buckley held the speed record on Windermere at 87 miles per hour. He was a close friend to Sir Donald Campbell who held the water speed record on Coniston Water at nearly 300 miles per hour.

Impact Management Training Company founded 30 years ago took over the house for their business 25 years ago.

Desmond Yare helped the previous chef at Cragwood in 2002 and took the reigns in the kitchen in 2007. With a career wealth of knowledge of all types of cuisine from Michelin star to bistro.

Having worked alongside such well known chefs as Raymond Blanc, Bruno Loubet and Marco Pierre White sourcing local produce for "Farm to Fork" dining has been Des's goal.

In his accomplished kitchen brigade, second in command Calvin, with help from Chris and Lawrence maintain Desmond's desire for fine food: Alongside them Kate our resident chocolate specialist and speciality cake maker.

For a dining experience for two, your wedding reception or christening, Desmond and his team excel to meet your demands.

Having worked alongside such well known chefs as Raymond Blanc, Bruno Loubet and Marco Pierre White, sourcing local produce for "Farm to Fork" dining has been Des's goal

SMOKED DUCK, BEETROOT RELISH, DEEP FRIED DUCK EGG, TRUFFLE DRESSING

ONE DUCK BREAST SERVES 2

Ingredients

1 Breast Smoked Duck

Beetroot Relish

1 kg grated beetroot
200g finely sliced white cabbage
25g fresh horseradish
15g English mustard powder
200g malt vinegar
20g cayenne pepper
100g demerara sugar

Deep Fried Duck Egg

100g seasoned flour (salt and pepper)
1 hens egg (whisked)
100g fresh bread crumbs
1 duck egg

Truffle Dressing

50ml balsamic vinegar
100ml truffle oil

Method

Fot the beetroot relish

Put cabbage, grated beetroot, fresh horseradish, mustard powder, sugar, vinegar, and cayenne pepper in a saucepan. Cook until tender and completely reduced. Cool and store in jars. Refrigerate.

For the deep fried duck egg

Simmer water with a touch of vinegar and salt. Poach duck egg for 1-½ minutes then refresh into iced water. Gently drain and dry. Coat the poached egg in seasoned flour, then coat in the whisked egg and finally coat in breadcrumbs. Deep fry until golden brown.

For the truffle dressing

Mix truffle oil and balsamic vinegar together and whisk.

To serve

Slice the duck breast and present as shown in the photograph.

SADDLE OF RABBIT STUFFED WITH MERGUEZ CONFIT TOMATO

ONE SADDLE SERVES 1

Ingredients

1 Saddle Boned (ask butcher to do this)

Confit of Tomato

4 vine tomatoes
icing sugar
sea salt
fresh thyme
olive oil

Quinoa

200g quinoa (a grain from South America)
1 stick of celery
1 peeled carrot
1 peeled shallot
500ml chicken stock

Smoked Garlic Foam

4 peeled cloves of garlic
1 Merguez sausage (a Moroccan sausage)
200ml milk
wood chippings (from a specialised butcher)

Method

For the confit of tomato

Peel and deseed tomatoes and sprinkle with a little icing sugar and a little sea salt. Add a touch of thyme then dribble with olive oil. Leave to infuse for 2 hours in a warm place.

For the quinoa

Dice the shallot, carrot and celery in to fine dice, sweat in a touch of olive oil and add Quinoa and chicken stock. Cook until tender to touch. Cool and refrigerate.

For the saddle of rabbit

Lie the boned rabbit flat, line the tomato confit where the bone was removed and also add the Merguez sausage. Wrap up and tie to cook on gas mark 5 for 10 minutes.

For the smoked garlic foam

Blanch the garlic, cool and then place in a saucepan with the wood chippings, cover and cook for 2 minutes.

Keep covered so the garlic takes the flavour, add to warm milk and strain through a fine sieve. Whisk till foam.

To serve

Present as shown in the photograph.

WARM CHOCOLATE FONDANT, PISTACHIO ANGLAISE AND MILK ICE CREAM

CHOCOLATE FONDANT SERVES 8

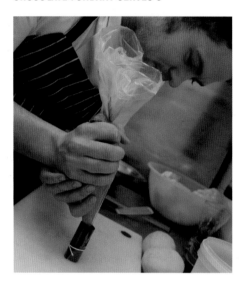

Method

For the chocolate fondant

Grease metal ring with butter and cocoa powder then place onto a tray with silicone paper and refrigerate. Melt the butter and chocolate pistols, whisk eggs and yolk and 250g sugar until stiff. Gently fold chocolate mixture and 130g flour; gently fill the greased mould about half full. Refrigerate until needed.

For the pistachio anglaise

Heat the 400ml of cream and pistachio paste, mix yolks and caster sugar, pour on the boiled cream and return to the heat. Gently cook till it coats back of the wooden spoon.

For the milk ice cream

Boil 500ml milk, 500ml cream and 400ml condensed milk. Add to this 16 yolks and 300g sugar, mix together and pour onto the boiled milk and cream. Mix together and chill. Then churn in an ice cream machine and freeze.

To serve

Cook chocolate fondant for 10 minutes on gas mark 5 and present as shown in photograph.

Ingredients

Chocolate Fondant

metal ring 1½ inch x 2 inch

300g melted dark chocolate pistol (58% cocoa)
250g unsalted butter
4 eggs
5 yolks
250g caster sugar
130g plain flour (sieved)

Pistachio Anglaise

1 dessert spoon of pistachio paste
6 yolks
100g caster sugar
400ml cream

Milk Ice Cream

500ml milk
500ml whipping cream
400ml condensed milk
16 yolks
300g sugar

38
DALE LODGE HOTEL

Red Bank Road, Grasmere, Cumbria LA22 9SW

015394 35300
www.dalelodgehotel.co.uk

The success of Dale Lodge Hotel is a result of passion and ambition from the family who own and operate it. Much work has been undertaken to build a reputation of quality service and excellent food. The building and its decor have undergone dramatic changes from an old fashioned, traditional place to something contemporary, clean and spacious with the extended Tweedies Bar going from strength to strength.

The food which is passionately created by head chef James Goodall is of a classic style with a continental twist. James trained in London from the age of 16 before working in France, Spain and Australia where he gained some excellent experience and masses of inspiration which comes through in his work today. He returned to his home in the Lake District in 2002 and before opening Dale Lodge, was head chef at The Log House Restaurant in Ambleside.

In Tweedies Bar our full menu is available in more informal surroundings. With a large range of award winning real ales, extensive wine list and possibly the largest beer garden in The Lake District, Tweedies Bar is a wonderful place for a light lunch, family gathering or special occasion.

The more intimate setting of The Lodge Restaurant is set within the main hotel where the sumptuous surroundings, flickering candlelight and personal service make for a perfect and memorable evening.

With a large range of award winning real ales, extensive wine list and possibly the largest beer garden in The Lake District, Tweedies Bar is a wonderful place for a light lunch, family gathering or special occasion.

BLUE CHEESE AND RED ONION TART

SERVES 4

Ingredients

For The Pastry

500g plain flour
250g butter
a pinch of salt
water to consistency

For The Filling

500g sliced blue cheese (any blue cheese is fine
but Blacksticks Blue is our preference)
5 medium sized red onions
300ml red wine
1 heaped tbsp demerara sugar
25ml olive oil

To Garnish

200ml ruby port
150ml olive oil
salt and pepper
1 Cox's Pippin apple
4 sticks of celery and leaves
100g walnuts
100g radish (washed and sliced)

Method

For the tart cases

Rub the flour, butter and salt together, add water a little at a time until it reaches a satisfactory consistency.
Refrigerate overnight.

Flour a cold surface and roll out your pastry circles 2 inches wider than your tart cases and about ½ cm thick.

Grease the tart cases with a little butter, roll the pastry back onto your rolling pin and gently lay it into the cases, making sure you don't get any holes in it.

Fill the cases with some rice or beans wrapped in clingfilm to prevent the pastry from rising or bubbling and bake in a pre-heated oven at 170°C for about 10 minutes.

Remove the rice from the tart case and bake for a further 5 minutes.

For the filling

First peel and finely slice the red onions.

Soften the onions in a little oil over a medium heat.

Add the sugar, then the red wine and cook gently for 20 minutes until it binds together.

Put a quarter of the onion marmalade and then a quarter of the sliced cheese in each tart case.

Place on a tray lined with greaseproof paper and bake in a pre-heated oven until the cheese melts.

To make the vinaigrette combine the port and olive oil and whisk gently by hand to form a loose emulsion. Season to taste with salt and pepper.

Peel, wash and slice the apple, radish, celery and celery leaves, then dress with the walnuts and port vinaigrette.

PAN FRIED SEA BASS WITH SPRING VEGETABLES AND A LEMON BEURRE BLANC

SERVES 4

Ingredients

4 sea bass fillets
16 equally sized salad potatoes
spinach (washed and picked)
100g radish (washed and sliced)
100g broad beans (washed and skinned)
100g baby leeks (washed and trimmed)

Beurre Blanc

500g diced unsalted butter
100ml double cream
2 shallots, roughly chopped
juice of ½ lemon
1 heaped tablespoon of finely chopped chives
100ml white wine vinegar
100ml white wine
1 sprig of thyme

Method

For the beurre blanc

Put the white wine vinegar, the white wine, shallots and the thyme into a pan and simmer gently until it has reduced by half, then pass through a fine sieve and discard the excess.

Add the cream, then the diced butter a little at a time whilst whisking continuously on a low heat.

Add the chives, lemon juice, salt and pepper to taste.

For the vegetables

Put the potatoes in a pan of boiling water with a pinch of salt and cook on a medium heat for about 20 minutes then remove from the pan to cool.

Put 1tbsp olive oil in a pan on a medium heat, slice the potatoes about ½ an inch thick and sauté gently until golden brown.

Add the vegetables to the pan and continue to cook until the spinach has wilted and the leeks are softened.

Drain the vegetables on some kitchen roll to remove any excess water.

For the fish

Heat a non-stick pan with a little olive oil and place the sea bass skin side down in the pan.

Cook for three minutes then add a knob of butter and turn over.

Baste the fish with the butter in the pan and cook for a further 2 - 3 minutes.

Arrange the potatoes and vegetables in the bottom of a large bowl, gently place the fish on top and drizzle the beurre blanc over the vegetables to serve.

VANILLA PANNA COTTA

SERVES 4

Ingredients

2 gelatine leaves
400ml milk
1 vanilla pod
400ml double cream
100g sugar

Method

Soak the gelatine leaves in cold water to soften them.

Split open the vanilla pod and remove the seeds.

Put the cream, milk, and vanilla pod into a pan and bring it to the boil.

Remove the softened gelatine from the water and add it to the pan.

Add the sugar and allow the gelatine and sugar to dissolve, keep stirring and remove it from the heat.

Pass the mixture through a fine sieve to remove the vanilla pod and make it extra smooth.

Allow the mixture to cool and thicken a little, giving it an occasional stir.

Pour it into individual moulds and then refrigerate for at least 6 hours before serving.

Turn the panna cottas out onto a plate. If they stick try pouring a little warm water over the bottom of the moulds.

Serve them with a little fruit coulis and some fresh fruit to garnish.

48
FAYRER GARDEN HOUSE HOTEL

Lyth Valley Road, Bowness on Windermere, Cumbria LA23 3JP

015394 88195
www.fayrergarden.com

Built in 1904, this beautiful Lakeland Country House was a former Edwardian gentlemen's residence set in five acres of secluded beautiful gardens and grounds. Today Fayrer Garden offers all the style and elegance you would expect from a three-star country house hotel. The welcoming ambience is evident from the moment you step over the threshold – the atmosphere is most definitely relaxed.

With unrivalled views of Lake Windermere and the surrounding countryside, the Terrace Restaurant has a well established reputation for fine food. Our skilled kitchen team lead by Chef Edward Wilkinson for the last 15 years, produce daily changing menus to reflect both the season and the best ingredients the region has to offer.

Stylish lounges offer views across the terrace and the Lake beyond where morning coffee or afternoon tea can be enjoyed. The cosy bar invites you to sit and relax with an aperitif or indeed a night-cap allowing you to sample one of our many single malts or local bottled real ales. The colourful gardens with their eye-catching borders have received many awards over the years. The spacious terrace is a wonderful place to sit and enjoy the peace and tranquillity.

All the bedrooms have views – either over Lake Windermere or of the attractive gardens. The bedrooms are all individually designed to the highest of standards

– no two are the same! Ground floor rooms have patio doors to allow direct access onto the terrace whilst all the first floor Lake View rooms enjoy the added luxury of a whirlpool bath.

A stunning spa and leisure club at a neighbouring hotel is available for guests to use and Windermere Golf Club is only a mile up the road. The nearby village of Bowness with all its shops, attractions and boats is a brisk 15 minute walk.

Good food and fine wines, stylish lounges and luxurious accommodation have become the hotels trademarks. Let the staff help you unwind – you may well become one of our many guests who return time after time.

Gayl
Garden
HOUSE HOTE

The Terrace
Restaurant

AA ★★★

Rosettes for fine food

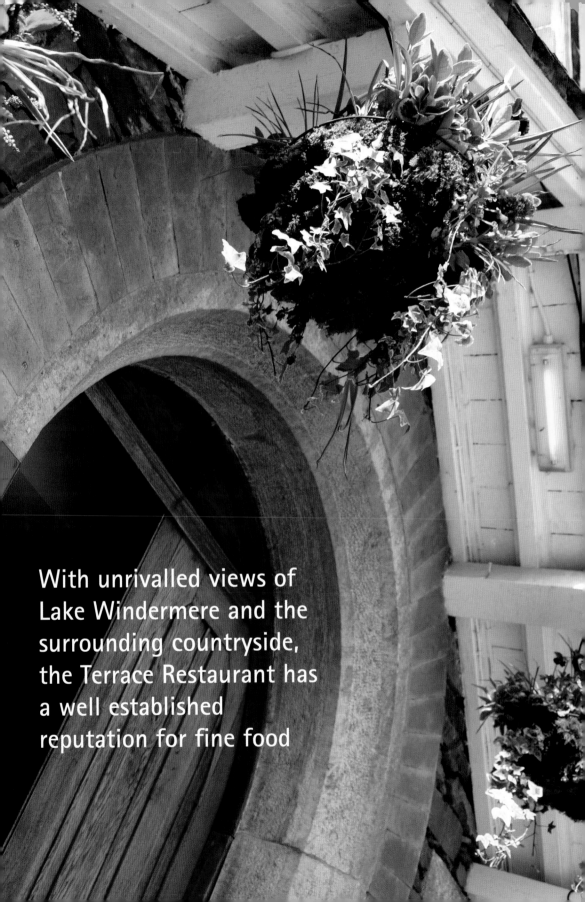

With unrivalled views of
Lake Windermere and the
surrounding countryside,
the Terrace Restaurant has
a well established
reputation for fine food

PAN FRIED CARTMEL VALLEY PIGEON WITH ONION TART AND SWEET POTATO TERRINE

SERVES 4

Ingredients

4 plump pigeon breasts
½ tsp chopped thyme
½ orange, juiced

Caramelised Onion Tart

2 onions (red or white)
2 whole eggs
¼ pint milk (or ½ milk / ½ cream mix)
salt and pepper to taste
4 small (2") pastry cases

Sweet Potato Terrine

1 lb sweet potato (peeled, chopped, boiled in
salted water and drained well)
6 whole eggs
1 pint double cream

Redcurrant and Port Reduction

8 fl oz port (use a ruby or LBV)
120g good quality redcurrant jelly
1 pint demi glace (or good quality beef stock)
1 onion (finely chopped)
1 tsp olive oil

Method

Marinate the pigeon breasts in the juiced orange and thyme and keep in the fridge until required.

For the tart

Slice the onions thinly and cook in a little oil until brown and well cooked. Divide between the pastry cases taking care not to over-fill.

Whisk the eggs, milk mixture and seasoning together and then pour over the pastry cases until just full.

Cook in a medium oven for around 15 – 20 minutes until set.

For the terrine

Place all ingredients in a food blender and puree until smooth. Sieve and check seasoning.

Pour into a cling film lined terrine mould and cover. Place the mould in a large baking dish and fill with water. Bake in the Bains Marie for about 2 hours in a medium oven or until the terrine is set though.

To prepare the dish for serving

Heat a frying pan until hot, melt about a tsp of butter with a tsp of oil and then fry the breasts for 5 minutes on each side. Ideally the middle should be pink. Leave to rest on one side for a few minutes.

Slice the terrine and place on a baking sheet with the onion tarts and warm in the oven.

Place the pigeon to one side of a warm plate, onion tart in the middle and sweet potato terrine on the other side. Serve with the redcurrant and port reduction.

Redcurrant and port reduction

Heat the olive oil in a heavy based pan and add the onion. Cook gently until soft.

Add the port and the redcurrant jelly and cook until reduced by two-thirds.

Add the demi glaze / stock and reduce the quantity of the pan by half to be left with a rich jus to accompany the pigeon.

GRILLED FILLET OF SEA BASS, CONFIT OF FENNEL AND TOMATO, WARM SHRIMPS, TOMATO COULIS

SERVES 4

Ingredients

Sea Bass

4 large fillets of sea bass

1 tsp olive oil
salt and pepper to taste
½ lemon

Fennel and Tomato Confit

2 fist sized bulbs of fennel
1 beef tomato (or 3 salad tomatoes)
splash white wine

Warm Shrimps

½ lb good quality brown shrimp
or prawns
½ tsp chopped chives
½ tsp chopped parsley
½ tsp lemon juice
salt and pepper to taste

Tomato Coulis

2 – 3 beef tomatoes (6 – 8 salad tomatoes)
½ onion (finely chopped)
½ tsp garlic puree / chopped garlic
olive oil
splash white wine
caster sugar, salt and pepper to taste

Method

For the sea bass

When ready to serve, grill the seabass with a little of the olive oil, seasoning to taste and a squeeze of lemon juice. It should only take a couple of minutes to cook the fillets on a medium heat grill.

For the fennel and tomato confit

Remove the core and leaves of the fennel and then thinly slice.

In a saucepan, cook the fennel with a good splash of white wine and some seasoning. Cook until al-dente.

Meanwhile, peel and de-seed the tomato. Finely chop the flesh to make the concasse. Add this to the fennel and cook for a further 10 minutes.

For the warm shrimps

Make sure the shrimps are clean and fresh. Mix all the ingredients together and keep in the refrigerator until the last minute.

Just before serving, warm the shrimps in a dry saucepan just to take the chill off them.

For the tomato coulis

Peel, de-seed and finely chop the remaining tomato flesh. Keep to one side.

Cook the onion in a saucepan with a little olive oil until soft but not browned.

Add the tomato, garlic and a good splash of white wine. Boil and reduce by half.

Season with salt and pepper to taste and if required add a little sugar. Cook for a further 10 minutes.

Liquidize the mixture and then pass through a fine sieve. Check seasoning again and keep warm.

To serve

Place the fennel and tomato confit in the centre of the plate.

Serve the grilled sea bass on top of this and then spoon the warm shrimps over the sea bass.

Finish the plate off by drizzling the sauce around the side.

CHOCOLATE TRUFFLE MOUSSE

SERVES 6 - 8

Method

To make the Genoise sponge

Whisk the eggs thoroughly and then add the sugar. Continue to whisk until double in size. Fold in the flour using a metal spoon and when fully incorporated, add the melted butter.

Spread onto silicone paper or a well greased baking tray. The mixture only needs to be ¼ inch thick.

Bake in a medium – hot oven for about 7 – 10 minutes. When cooked remove paper, cool and use as the base for the mousse.

For the mousse

Gently heat the cream on the hob, adding the chocolate, stirring occasionally.

Whip the egg yolks with the sugar until light and double in size.

With the cream and chocolate mixture thoroughly combined and just off the boil, add the egg mixture and stir in well. The mixture will thicken at this stage and you can add a flavouring here if you like - a splash of Grand Marnier for example.

Put the tin on top of the sponge and press to make the bottom seal. Pour the mixture into the tin and refrigerate for a minimum of 5 hours.

Serve a slice of the truffle mousse with a good quality raspberry sorbet and tuile biscuit.

To make the biscuits

Mix the egg whites with the sugar, add the flour and then add the melted butter. Mix well and chill. Cut a shape i.e. rectangle or triangle out of a thin piece of plastic or cardboard.

Spread the tuille mixture using a palate knife thinly over the cut-out onto a baking tray lined with parchment to produce very thin strip of mixture.

Cook in a medium oven until golden brown. When cooked, slide off the tray using a palette knife and drape over a rolling pin to 'curve' the biscuit. Leave to cool.

Grand Marnier sauce

Heat the cream and milk in a heavy bottomed saucepan until just to the boil. Meanwhile, whisk the yolks with the corn flour until smooth and add the sugar. Continue to whisk until all ingredients are nearly smooth.

When the milk has just boiled remove from the heat, and add the egg mixture to the mix whisking the milk vigorously at the same time. The residual heat from the pan should thicken the mixture and cook the sauce sufficiently not to require any further heating.

Add Grand Marnier to taste and leave to cool. Serve with the Chocolate Mousse.

Ingredients

For The Mousse

680g dark chocolate
1 pint double cream
120g caster sugar
4 egg yolks

For The Genoise Base

6 eggs
170g caster sugar
170g plain flour (sifted)
85g melted butter

Tuille Biscuit

2 egg whites
120g caster sugar
60g melted butter
60g plain flour

Grand Marnier Sauce

6 egg yolks
½ pint double cream
½ pint whole milk
60g caster sugar
1 tbsp cornflour
splash Grand Marnier

58
GILPIN LODGE HOTEL

Crook Road, Windermere, Cumbria LA23 3NE

01539 488 818
www.gilpinlodge.co.uk

Voted England's Best Small Hotel 2010 by Visit Britain, Gilpin Lodge Hotel has been privately owned and run by the Cunliffe family since 1987 and is a member of Relais and Chateaux. Along with their long established team, Gilpin has developed a certain style, which encourages guests to return again and again.

Service is personal, professional but relaxed. Interiors are stunning but cosy and each room is very different and shown in detail on their website at www.gilpinlodge.co.uk. Most of the 20 bedrooms in the hotel are suites and many lead directly out onto 20 acres of beautiful gardens, many with their own private hot tubs. Gilpin Lake House suites enjoy stunning views over a private lake with exclusive use of 100 acres of grounds with spa, boathouse, summerhouse, kitchen gardens and wonderful walks within the grounds with fabulous views.

The AA 3-rosette restaurant has 4 intimate dining rooms and the menu is a celebration of the Lake District's finest produce and West Coast seafood. Dishes range from classic favourites to contemporary surprises. The head chef, Russell Plowman, joined Gilpin in 2009 after long spells developing his skills at the Michelin starred L'Orlotan and The Waterside Inn at Bray.

Gilpin is located just 2 miles from Windermere, at the very centre of the lakes but hidden from the crowds.

The Gilpin Lake House

Opened in 2010, the Gilpin Lake House is the ultimate Lake District escape. Set in 100 acres of grounds and on the shore a private 4 acre lake, the 6 suites will have exclusive use of a spa (swimming pool, sauna, hot tub, treatments), summerhouse, boathouse, druids circle, gardens and walks. From the conservatory, watch wild ducks at play on the lake during breakfast and afternoon tea, and then by chauffeur arrive at the hotel restaurant for dinner.

TWICE BAKED STICHELTON CHEESE SOUFFLÉ, WALDORF SALAD, RED WINE REDUCTION

SERVES 6

Ingredients

Soufflé

250g mild cheddar
250g Stichelton cheese (or other medium
strength blue cheese)
250g butter
250g plain flour
1 tsp Dijon mustard
500g egg white

Waldorf Salad

1 Granny Smith apple
10 shelled walnut halves
100g green seedless grapes peeled
4 large shallots sliced
1 head of celery sliced
500ml red wine
100g sugar
1 star anise
1 cinnamon stick
4 cloves

Red Wine Reduction

500ml red wine
500ml ruby port
1 cinnamon stick
1 star anise
4 cloves

Method

For the soufflé

Melt the butter in a saucepan and add the plain flour. Cook
out the flour for 5 minutes before adding the milk. Cook the mix
for 20 minutes and take off the heat. In a food processor, mix
the sauce with the grated cheeses and add the Dijon mustard,
salt and pepper. Blend until a smooth mix has been achieved.
Butter 6 ramekins and line with some crushed walnuts. Whisk
the egg whites until soft peaks and fold into the cheese mix.
Fill the lined ramekins with the soufflé base and bake in a
preheated oven set at 180°C for 7 minutes, then turn the
ramekins and cook for a further 7 minutes. Leave to cool
before removing from the ramekins.

For the Waldorf salad

Make syrup by bringing to a boil the red wine with the sugar and
spices and pour over the grapes and shallots. Leave to marinade
for 24 hours to absorb the flavour of the marinade and colour.

Arrange the sliced celery on the plate and top with some of the
apple, walnuts, grapes and shallot.

Meanwhile reheat the soufflés in the oven set at 180°C for
7 minutes and serve immediately.

For the Red wine reduction

Bring to a boil the alcohol with the spices and slowly reduce
until syrupy. Strain the syrup and use to dress the soufflés.

ROASTED BEST END AND BRAISED SHOULDER OF HERDWICK LAMB, GARLIC AND POTATO PURÉE, ROSEMARY SAUCE

SERVES 6

Ingredients

600g boned shoulder of lamb
2 ltr lamb stock
150g butter
2 shallots
1 carrot
2 heads of garlic
400g trimmed lamb best end
50ml olive oil

Garlic and Potato Puree

3kg Desiree potatoes
100g coarse rock salt
250ml whipping cream
4 cloves of garlic
200g unsalted butter

Method

For the lamb

Start the preparation a day in advance. In a heavy based frying pan caramelize the boned and rolled lamb shoulder to a deep golden brown colour in a little vegetable oil. Once browned, remove from the pan and roast the carrot, shallot and garlic before adding to the lamb shoulder. Cover in lamb stock, bring to a boil and skim. Put in an oven set at 150°C and cook slowly for 3 to 4 hours until the meat is tender. Roughly flake and allow to cool, but while the meat is still warm, roll the flakes tightly in cling film to form a large cylinder and slice into disks when cold. Reduce the stock to a sauce consistency.

To cook the best end caramelize the lamb in olive oil and cook in the oven for 6 minutes. Leave to rest before carving. Reheat the lamb shoulder in the sauce and serve.

For the garlic and potato purée

Prick the potatoes and bake on a bed of rock salt at 150°C for 1½ to 2 hours. Scoop out the flesh from the potatoes and pass with a fine sieve. Bring the cream to a boil with the butter and garlic and strain onto the dry potato purée. Mix together to achieve a smooth paste and season with salt and pepper.

RHUBARB AND CUSTARD
POACHED YORKSHIRE RHUBARB, VANILLA PANNA COTTA, RHUBARB SORBET

SERVES 6

Method

For the rhubarb

Put the water, sugar and vanilla in a large flat-bottomed saucepan and bring to a light boil. Reduce the heat to a simmer and add the rhubarb batons and poach very slowly at 150°C in the oven. Remove from the heat and cool in a large shallow container.

For the sorbet

Puree half of the poached rhubarb adding a little of the poaching liquid to achieve a smooth consistency and reserve in the fridge until required. For the sorbet mix, take half of the pureed rhubarb and mix with 800g stock syrup and a squeeze of lemon juice. Freeze in a sorbet machine.

For the panna cotta

Soften the gelatine in cold water. Bring to a boil the milk and cream and dissolve the sugar. Add the vanilla seeds and pour onto the softened gelatine, whisk until smooth. Pour into small ramekin moulds and leave to set on the fridge.

To serve

Decorate the plate with the rhubarb puree and place the poached rhubarb pieces on top. In 1 corner of the plate take out the panna cotta by lightly running it under warm water and place. Spoon the rhubarb sorbet in the other corner and garnish with some lightly roasted nuts and some sprigs of fennel.

Ingredients

Rhubarb and Custard

poached Yorkshire rhubarb, vanilla panna cotta, rhubarb sorbet

Rhubarb Poaching Liquor

2 kg pink forced Yorkshire rhubarb peeled and cut into 4cm batons
800g water
300g caster sugar
4g vanilla pods

Vanilla Panna Cotta

500ml milk
200ml whipping cream
2 vanilla pods scraped seeds removed
4 leaves gelatine
200g caster sugar

68
THE GLASS HOUSE RESTAURANT

Rydal Road, Ambleside, Cumbria LA22 9AN

01539 432 137
www.theglasshouserestaurant.co.uk

The Glass House Restaurant in Ambleside, lies at the centre of this most beautiful corner of England and at its culinary heart. The restaurant occupies a cleverly restored Grade 11 listed building dating from the 15th Century that operated as a fulling mill. When the mill was refurbished in 1995, the working weir, millrace, wheel and various pieces of machinery were carefully retained and an impressive oak framework was introduced to provide a series of imaginative mezzanine floors.

As for food, we use the freshest local produce from Lakeland fells and farms, and fuse classic British dishes with European menus. Freshness, quality and simplicity are our signature qualities. Our ingredients are always the best.

Atmosphere may not be edible but it does play a huge part in your dining enjoyment at the Glass House. Our friendly team serve in a refreshingly casual but attentive way to produce a relaxed, enjoyable ambience.

Head chef Richard Collins and second chef Daniel Hogben

When the mill was refurbished in 1995, the working weir, millrace, wheel and various pieces of machinery were carefully retained and an impressive oak framework was introduced to provide a series of imaginative mezzanine floors

PAN FRIED MACKEREL WITH HORSERADISH POTATO SALAD

SERVES 2

Ingredients

mackerel fillets
170g cooked new potatoes
2 tbsp mayonnaise
1 tbsp grated fresh horseradish
1 tbsp chopped chives
salad leaf

Method

Dice new potatoes and fold in mayonnaise and chives.

Pan fry mackerel fillets in olive oil and butter, 1 minute each side.

Place mackerel over potato salad and garnish with salad leaf.

ROAST BELLY PORK WITH APPLE POTATO CAKE AND CAULIFLOWER PURÉE

SERVES 6

Ingredients

boned belly pork with skin on
250g cooked new potatoes
125g peeled chopped apple
250g sliced red onion
50ml balsamic vinegar
25g dark brown sugar
1 head cauliflower, chopped
1pt water
1pt milk
salt
500g chopped onion, carrot, celery
1 medium garlic
rosemary/thyme
150ml cream

Method

For the pork

Pre heat oven to 130°C.

Place chopped vegetables in a deep roasting tray. Place pork on top and pour over the boiling water until pork is 3cm deep.

Season the pork with rosemary and thyme and cover with foil. Place in the oven to cook for 6 hours.

For the apple potato cake

Cook onions in a little oil and butter until soft and begin to colour. Add sugar and balsamic vinegar until mixture has thickened. Allow to cool.

Sauté apples and crush the warm new potatoes. Mix potato, onion and apple and press into a metal ring, leave to cool.

For the cauliflower purée

Cook cauliflower in milk and water, drain and blend until smooth.

Once pork is cooked, take off skin and return to oven at 180°C for 30 minutes until crispy.

Place baking tray on top of pork and weight down with something heavy for 1 hour, then cut into portions.

Reduce liquid from pork, skim fat and thicken.

To serve

Place pork and potato into oven at 180°C for 25 minutes.

Boil cream and stir in cauliflower purée.

Place crackling on top of potato cake; serve with the belly of pork and cauliflower purée to garnish.

STICKY TOFFEE PUDDING

SERVES 8

Ingredients

175g self raising flour
175g chopped dates
450ml boiling water
100g brown sugar
100g white sugar
65g soft butter
1 egg
1 tsp baking powder
1 tsp bicarbonate soda
½ tbsp ground cinnamon

Method

Soak dates in hot water.

Mix butter and sugar together until creamed.

Add flour, bicarbonate soda, baking powder and cinnamon and mix all together.

Add eggs.

Fold in dates and water.

Pour into a baking tray lined with greaseproof paper and cake at 160°C for 30 minutes.

78
JERICHOS

College Road, Windermere, Cumbria LA23 1BX

01539 442 522
www.jerichos.co.uk

Following twelve years of business Jerichos relocated into one of Windermere's original hotels, becoming a restaurant with rooms in 2008. The refurbished restaurant is located in a lovely Victorian building, in the heart of the village, with a welcoming ambience that reflects the mood, atmosphere and quality that Jerichos stands for. Whether you are visiting the restaurant for dinner or joining us for breakfast, Chris' passion for food is replicated in each dish he serves. The evening a la carte menu guarantees that each dish is brimming with great tastes, using in-season quality produce, and with frequent changes there is always something different to try.

Jerichos is exactly the sort of place my wife Jo and I wanted to create, a fantastic modern restaurant serving great food within a great Victorian building, full of character and charm, with the additional option of bedrooms.

The menu is always big on taste and very concise in length guaranteeing freshly cooked real food every time. The marriage of food and wine are important to us, so to complement the delicious food at Jerichos, we also have an extensive wine list giving you the opportunity to experience a global wealth of flavour, matched with food and our commitment to offering outstanding value for money. To make the choice easier try the "Wines of the month" or opt for our wine tasting selection, a pre- chosen wine with each course.

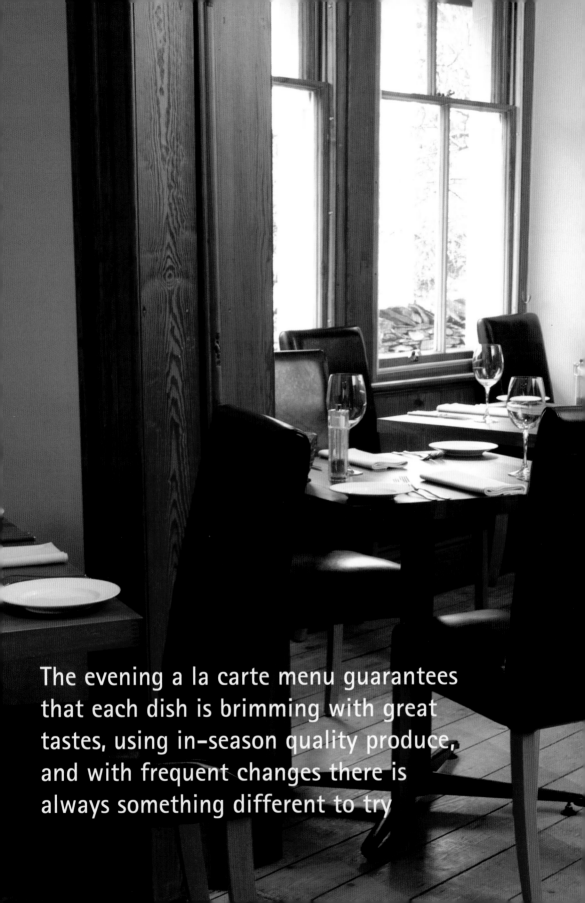

The evening a la carte menu guarantees
that each dish is brimming with great
tastes, using in-season quality produce,
and with frequent changes there is
always something different to try

PAN SEARED BREAST OF WOOD PIGEON WITH CARAMELISED ONION AND BLACK PUDDING

SERVES 4

Ingredients

Wood Pigeon

4 fresh wood pigeon breasts, off the bone
2 tbsp groundnut oil
salt and black pepper

For The Black Pudding

8 x 25g slices of black pudding stick
groundnut oil

Caramelised Onion

25g butter
2 onions, halved and sliced thinly
60g caster sugar
2 tbsp white wine vinegar

Red Pepper Fondue

1 red pepper diced (small)
1 tomato, chopped
100ml olive oil
½ shallot finely diced
1 garlic clove peeled and finely chopped
1 sprig of thyme

To Serve

chervil
balsamic syrup

Method

For the red pepper fondue

Place the oil in a small sauce pan and heat until simmering, carefully add the diced red pepper and lower the heat, cook for two minutes and then add the chopped tomato, followed by the garlic and thyme. Cook all until nice and soft and then liquidise and pass through a fine sieve, you should have a nice sauce consistency......if too thick just add a little boiling water until you get the consistency you need. This can be done ahead of time, stored in the fridge and re-heated when required.

For the onions

Melt the butter in a non stick pan and add the sliced onion, cook on a high heat until well browned. At this stage add the sugar and continue to cook on a medium heat until all the liquid has reduced, then add the vinegar and continue cooking until a marmalade consistency is achieved, remove from the heat. Again this can be done ahead of time and reheated when needed.

For the black pudding

Season and shallow fry in the groundnut oil until piping hot all the way through.

For the woodpigeon breasts

Place the oil in a non stick frying pan and heat until just smoking, carefully place the breasts one at a time into the oil skin side down and cook until nicely browned, turn over and turn off the heat, the heat of the pan will continue to cook the wood pigeon, the best way to serve is nicely pink, you need to check to get to the stage you prefer.

To assemble the dish

Place some warm caramelised onion in the centre of each plate followed by a slice of black pudding, then some more onion, another piece of black pudding and then a little more onion. Remove the pigeon from the pan and slice thinly onto the top of the black pudding tower. Spoon the red pepper fondue and balsamic syrup in thin circles around the tower and garnish with fresh sprigs of chervil.

LOIN OF LAKELAND LAMB WITH CREAMED POTATOES AND RATATOUILLE

SERVES 4

Ingredients

Lamb

4 x 120g portions lamb loin eye meat,
off the bone and skinned
1 tbsp sunflower/grapeseed oil
salt and black pepper

Ratatouille

2 red peppers, chopped into small dice
2 courgettes, chopped into small dice
1 small aubergine, chopped into small dice
1 small onion, diced
2 tbsp olive oil
1 tin chopped plum tomatoes, better than fresh
for this!!!
6 fresh basil leaves, torn into pieces
salt and black pepper

For The Creamed Potatoes

500g peeled, diced Maris Piper potatoes
1 medium onion, diced
1 tbsp olive oil
4 sprigs rosemary, green strands removed and
finely chopped
150ml double cream
salt and black pepper

Fine Green Beans

125g fine green beans

Method

For the ratatouille

Place the onions and olive oil in a pan and cook until slightly browned, add the diced red peppers and cook for a further 3 or 4 minutes until softened and then add the diced courgettes and diced aubergine and cook for a further 3-4 minutes stirring all the time. Add the tin of chopped tomatoes and cook on a medium heat until the juice in the pan is reduced down and you have slightly sticky, colourful ratatouille, at this stage fold in the torn basil leaves and season to taste. Put to one side.

For the potatoes

Place the potatoes in a pan of simmering salted water and cook until al dente, cooked through but not falling to mush, drain in a sieve and leave to one side. When fully drained place back in the pan. Meanwhile in a small frying pan place the diced onion and olive oil and cook until translucent, add the chopped rosemary and stir for 1 minute, remove from the heat and add to the potatoes. Add the double cream, season to taste, heat and stir gently until you get to a lumpy mashed potato consistency, keep warm.

For the beans

Cook the French beans in boiling salted water, drain, place back into the pan, season and add a small knob of butter, keep warm.

For the lamb

Place the oil in a non stick frying pan and heat until it just starts to smoke. Turn down the heat, season and carefully place the lamb loins one at a time into the oil and pan fry on both sides until well browned, continue to cook until you reach the stage at which you prefer to eat your lamb, this is trial by error I'm afraid.

To assemble the dish

Place a spoonful of the creamed rosemary potatoes into the centre of each plate and on top of this a generous spoonful of ratatouille followed by the glazed French beans, remove the lamb from the pan, slice across the loin and place on top of the beans and finally pour over and around the red wine sauce.

LEMON TART

SERVES 8

Ingredients

Sweet Pastry

230g very soft butter (not clarified)
2 large eggs
450g plain flour
60g icing sugar sieved

Lemon Tart

1 sweet pastry base baked blind
(20cm x 3.75cm deep)
5 lemons
8 large eggs
400g caster sugar
250ml double cream

To Serve

1 large punnet fresh raspberries
50ml raspberry purée
mint

Method

For the pastry

Place butter in a large bowl, followed by the flour, icing sugar and lastly the eggs. Bring all together gently by hand until soft and malleable and all flour incorporated.

Divide into 4 equal portions, cover and chill for at least 1 hour.

Before using the pastry, allow to soften at room temperature (think soft plasticine).

For the tart

Have ready the pastry base, baked blind using the sweet pastry and checked for holes. Finely grate the zest and squeeze the juice from all of the lemons making sure to remove the pips.

Whisk the eggs and sugar together thoroughly in a bowl, then add the lemon juice and zest. Stir in the cream.

Pour the lemon mixture into the pastry case and cook in a preheated oven at 130ºC/260ºF for 30-40mins until the centre just starts to set.

Leave to rest for an hour and serve warm (still very good a day later too!!)

To serve

Portion the tart into eight equal portions and place one portion in the centre of each plate. To the side of the tart make a little pile of the fresh raspberries, about eight raspberries and spoon over some raspberry purée. Finally garnish with some fresh mint tips.

88
PURDEY'S RESTAURANT
AT THE LANGDALE ESTATE

The Langdale Estate, Great Langdale, Near Ambleside, Cumbria, LA22 9JD

01539 438 080
www.langdale.co.uk

Situated in the heart of the Lake District within the beautiful grounds of The Langdale Estate, Purdey's Restaurant is renowned for offering guests a true taste of Cumbria. Designed in the style of an old mill, with oak floors, local stone and views over the walled garden to the working waterwheel creates a relaxed yet interesting and unique dining experience. The original cannon, used to test gunpowder in the last century, is a reminder of the location's history.

Guided by the hand of experienced Executive Chef, Graham Harrower, the menu boasts stylish and imaginative Modern British dishes. An extensive wine list accompanies and complements the menu. Recently awarded the Sustainable Tourism Award by Cumbria Tourism, Langdale actively strives to provide a sustainable destination for visitors and the local community. In Purdey's this means top quality produce from the stunning hills and valleys all around minimizing the carbon footprint of our food and ensuring great tasting Lakeland food.

As well as Purdey's Restaurant, The Langdale Estate also offers one hundred timeshare and self catering properties, 56 luxury hotel bedrooms, the Terrace Restaurant, Spa and Wainwrights' Inn.

Great food, luxury accommodation and pampering spa treatments add up to a great experience all set in the heart of the Langdale Valley.

Guided by the hand of experienced Executive Chef, Graham Harrower, the menu boasts stylish and imaginative Modern British dishes. An extensive wine list accompanies and complements the menu

SEARED COD CHEEKS AND LANGOUSTINES, HAM HOCK TORTELLINI, CAULIFLOWER PUREE

SERVES 4

Ingredients

8 cod cheeks
8 langoustines shelled and de-veined
100g cooked and picked ham hock
100ml of reduced ham stock from braising
100g pasta
½ cauliflower
6 diced shallots
2 crushed garlic cloves
100g butter
100ml double cream
25g red amaranth

Method

Cauliflower puree, can be made in advance

Finely chop the cauliflower discarding the stalk, heat a saucepan and add 50g of butter, the cauliflower, garlic, half the shallots, cook over a low heat for 15 minutes taking care not to colour, once softened add half the cream and cook for another 5 minutes, blend in a food processor until smooth, taste and season then set aside until needed.

Ham hock tortellini, can be made in advance

Heat 50g of butter in a saucepan and add the shallots, cook until translucent. Add the ham hock and stir vigorously with a wooden spoon to break down to a paste, add the stock and reduce, take off the heat to cool slightly, once cooled roll the ham into small balls. Next take your pasta and roll out on a floured surface, as thin as possible (setting one if you have a pasta machine). Cut the pasta into circles 6cm in diameter, place the ham in the centre of the pasta circles, brush around the ham with cold water and fold pasta in half to create a semi-circle, next wet one point of the semi-circle and fold over again so both points are pressed together, with floured hands press firmly the point into the centre of the pasta.

Set aside until needed but do not cover with cling film.

To serve

Heat a heavy based frying pan, add a little oil, season the cod and langoustines, place in the pan, put the tortellini into boiling salted water. After 2 minutes turn the fish over then add 25g of butter to the oil, spoon the cooking juices back over the fish to enhance flavour, once cooked place fish and tortellini on a piece of kitchen cloth, plate the ingredients as shown in the photograph.

CUMBRIAN BEEF FILLET WITH OXTAIL AND TONGUE

SERVES 4

Ingredients

4 x 200g beef fillet portions
200g braised and picked oxtail
100g braised ox tongue
100ml beef jus
1 swede
200g washed baby spinach
100g unsalted butter
2 peeled baby onions
100g mashed potatoes
25g fresh horseradish
50g rolled pasta sheets
100ml double cream

Method

For the oxtail

Roll the oxtail into a long cylinder using cling film, cut into 2 inch pieces, wrap with the pasta sheets and roll again in cling film.

For the vegetables

Peel the swede and cut across so you have 1/2inch slices, using a 6cm cutter cut out 4 circles, boil in water and butter until soft. Sweat the trimmings down with butter and water until cooked and puree with a blender until smooth.

Heat the mashed potatoes in a sauce pan with the cream, add the grated horseradish, season to taste and keep warm.

For the beef fillet

In a very hot pan place the steaks in a little oil, season with salt and pepper, add the baby onions and cook in a moderate oven for 6 minutes turning half way through. When you take out the oven add a touch of butter and 4 pieces of ox tongue baste the steaks for 2 minutes then allow to rest for a few minutes before plating up.

Heat the oxtail in a pan of boiling water then plate up as shown in the photograph.

SOUS VIDE RHUBARB, MARSHMALLOW, GINGER BEER JELLY, RHUBARB SORBET

SERVES 6

Ingredients

Sous Vide Rhubarb

300g tender stem rhubarb
120g stock syrup
30g dry gin
juice of 1 lime
1 vanilla pod

Marshmallow

170g sugar
50g water
100g egg whites
1 ½ leaves soaked gelatine
1 vanilla pod

Ginger Beer Jelly

200g ginger beer
1 leaf soaked gelatine
20g sugar
juice of 1 lemon

Rhubarb Sorbet

500g rhubarb
125g caster sugar
15g liquid glucose
50g water
1 gelatine leaf
juice of ½ lemon

Rhubarb Purée

160g rhubarb
150g caster sugar
25g grenadine

Ginger Biscuits

125g butter
125g golden caster sugar
1 tbsp golden syrup
180g self raising flour
1 tsp ground ginger
1 egg yolk

Method

For the rhubarb

Cut the rhubarb into 7cm pieces and place in a vacuum bag.

Scrape the vanilla seeds into the stock syrup, gin and lime juice.

Pour the liquid into the bag and seal.

Poach the rhubarb in water at 60°C for 20 minutes.

Once cooked, plunge the bag into iced water to prevent further cooking.

For the marshmallow

Boil the sugar, water and vanilla until temperature reaches 118°C.

Add the gelatine.

Whip the egg whites in a mixer until they form soft peaks.

Turn the mixer down and slowly add the sugar syrup.

Continue to whip until the meringue has cooled and has thickened.

Pipe into moulds and set in the freezer.

For the ginger beer jelly

Boil the beer and sugar and then add the gelatine and lemon juice.

Set in the fridge.

For the rhubarb sorbet

Finely chop the rhubarb and place in a saucepan.

Add the glucose and water and bring to a simmer and cook for about 5 minutes until soft.

Add the soaked gelatine and blitz until smooth.

Freeze in a Paco Jet container for 24 hours before churning.

For the rhubarb puree

Finely chop the rhubarb and place in a saucepan.

Cover with the sugar and Grenadine and simmer for about 5 minutes until soft.

Blitz and pass through a fine mesh sieve.

For the ginger biscuits

Mix together the sugar, flour and ground ginger.

Melt the butter with the golden syrup.

Mix together with the egg yolk to form a soft dough.

Cover with cling film and leave to rest for 1 hour.

Make balls with the dough about the size of a 10p coin and place on greaseproof paper.

Bake on 180°C for 9-10 minutes.

RELISH CUMBRIA
PURDEY'S RESTAURANT AT THE LANGDALE ESTATE

MEREWOOD COUNTRY HOUSE HOTEL

Ecclerigg, Windermere, Cumbria LA23 1LH

01539 446 484
www.merewoodhotel.co.uk

Merewood is a country house hotel of great charm and distinction set in a position of incomparable scenic beauty.

The property was built in 1812 for the son of the 1st Earl of Lonsdale using stone quarried in the hotel grounds. The hotel retains many of its original features, including the beautifully panelled hall and reception rooms with glorious stained glass windows and magnificent fireplace, together with the silk-lined drawing room.

Standing in 20 acres of landscaped gardens, woodland and meadow, the terraced gardens fall towards the lake each revealing a new variation of the beautiful view of Lake Windermere. The hotel stands on its own secluded estate, and is easily accessible from the main route to and through the Lakes.

Merewood's friendly and efficient staff, the relaxed excellence of the service and the wonderful food served from Head Chef Leon Whitehead's kitchen are all of a quality to match the unparalleled location. It's easy to see why this hotel has become so popular with food lovers everywhere.

The Hotel is open all year including Christmas and New Year and the English Tourist Board has awarded it a "Highly Commended" three stars with silver accolade for food and service.

DMA Photography

The hotel retains many of its original features, including the beautifully panelled hall and reception rooms with glorious stained glass windows and magnificent fireplace, together with the silk-lined drawing room

PAN FRIED FILLET OF ORGANIC TROUT, CRAYFISH CANNELLONI, WILD GARLIC VELOUTE

SERVES 14

Ingredients

1 whole trout (1.5-2kg)
300g fresh pasta dough
olive oil
250g whiting fish fillets
175ml double dream
36 whole fresh crayfish
small amount of each – parsley, chives, chervil
5 shallots – extra finely diced
zest of 1 lemon
500ml fresh fish stock
250ml white wine
500ml double dream
300g wild garlic
50g butter

Method

For the trout

Descale the fish and fillet.

Pin bone the fillets, trim and portion.

For the cannelloni

Make fish mousse blending the whiting and pass through drum sieve, allow to chill.

Fold in 175ml double cream, season.

Chop herbs and add, plus finely grated zest of lemon.

Cook 2 of the finely diced shallots in a small amount of olive oil without colour.

Allow to cool and add to mousse mix.

Peel crayfish and reserve shells.

Finely dice crayfish tails and add to mousse mix and place into a piping bag.

Roll out pasta and cut into sheets about 10cm in length, blanch in boiling water and refresh in iced water. Dry sheets of pasta.

Pipe a cylinder of the filling across the pasta sheet and roll up into cannelloni shape.

Trim up the ends and cut length into 2, around 5cm each.

Place cannelloni onto a plate and cover with clingfilm.

For the sauce

Heat a small amount of olive oil in a thick-bottomed saucepan and fry remaining shallots.

Add shells from crayfish

Fry for couple of minutes and add white wine.

Reduce by a third.

Add fish stock and reduce by half.

Add double cream and reduce by half.

Pass liquid into clean pan and add chopped wild garlic.

Bring back to boil and place in a blender and blend until smooth.

Check seasoning and pass through a fine sieve.

To serve

Place cannelloni in steamer, and heat for 4/5 minutes.

Pan fry the trout in a non-stick pan and glaze with butter and season.

Heat sauce and pour into bowl.

Add the hot cannelloni and place the fish on top and serve.

ROASTED SADDLE OF HERDWICK LAMB AND CONFIT OF SHOULDER, CELERIAC PUREE, SPINACH, ROSEMARY SAUCE

SERVES 8

Ingredients

1 saddle of lamb – boned and lamb cannons removed
30g rock/sea salt
6 garlic cloves
2 litres duck fat
100g thyme
½ shoulder of lamb boned
4 maris piper potatoes
500g clarified butter
1 large celeriac
150ml double cream
150ml milk
100g unsalted butter
1kg baby spinach – washed

For The Sauce

trimmings from the lamb
1 litre lamb stock
½ litre brown chicken stock
3 cloves of garlic – chopped
4 shallots – thinly sliced
50ml olive oil
150ml madeira
150ml red wine
50g rosemary

Method

For the confit of shoulder

Trim shoulder of any sinew and skin.

Chop thyme and garlic and mix well with salt.

Rub into shoulder and leave in a fridge overnight.

Heat duck fat to 70°C.

Add lamb and confit for 5-6 hours.

When cooked remove from the fat and roll into a firm cylinder using cling film, about 4/5cm in diameter.

Place in fridge until firm, then slice into 10mm slices.

Brown in a little duck fat and keep warm.

For the lamb cannon

Trim the cannons of sinew and portion into 4, from each cannon.
Reserve the trimmings for the sauce.

For the potato galette

Peel and julienne potato, mix with a little clarified butter

Shape on a metal tray using large round pastry cutter, then bake in the oven 180°C until golden brown , keep warm.

For the sauce

Heat oil in a saucepan and add lamb trimmings, shallots and garlic, cook until golden.

Add madeira and red wine and reduce until a glaze.

Add chopped rosemary, and both stocks.

Bring to the boil and simmer for 30 minutes.

Pass through a fine sieve into a clean pan and reduce to 400ml.

Season and keep warm.

For the celeriac fondants and puree

Peel celeriac and slice into four and cut out 16 small rounds.

Lightly brown tops of celeriac rounds and cover with clarified butter and cook on a low heat until soft, keep warm.

Chop the remaining celeriac and place in a pan with the cream and milk and simmer until the celeriac is soft.

Transfer the celeriac mix to a blender and blend until smooth.

Add butter a bit at a time and correct the seasoning.

To serve

Brown the lamb cannons and roast in a hot oven for 3 minutes.

Allow to rest and then slice.

Cook the spinach and season and assemble dish as in picture.

BRAMLEY APPLE CRUMBLE WITH ENGLISH CIDER BRANDY CREAM, GRANNY SMITH'S APPLE SORBET

SERVES 10

Ingredients

Apple Mix

1 lemon
2 kg Bramley apples
2 vanilla pods
350g caster sugar
75g unsalted butter

Crumble Topping

300g plain flour
150g granulated sugar
pinch cinnamon
150g cold butter

Granny Smith's Apple Sorbet

10 Granny Smith apples
200ml apple juice
juice 2 lemons
stock syrup - 20° baume
pinch ascorbic acid

Croquant Baskets

240g sugar
80g confectioners glucose
200g nibbed almonds

English Cider Brandy Cream

200ml double cream
25ml cider brandy
25g caster sugar

Method

For the sorbet

In a thermo mix blend apples (leave skin on).

Add apple juice, lemon juice, ascorbic acid.

Squeeze mix through double layer of muslin, into a jug.

Using a saccharometer add stock syrup until reaches 20° Baume.

Place into ice cream machine and churn until frozen.

For the crumble mix

Place all ingredients into food processor and blitz for about 10 seconds or until you get a breadcrumb texture.

For the apple mix

Juice lemon into bowl of cold water.

Peel, core and dice apples, around 2cm in size.

Place in saucepan with scraped vanilla pods, sugar and butter.

Cook until nice and soft but still retaining a little shape.

Remove from heat and spoon mixture into lined rings, leaving 1½cm for crumble topping.

Once crumble topping is on place into oven and bake for 25minutes at 200°C .

For the croquant basket

Make caramel with sugar and glucose.

Remove from heat and add almonds.

Pour onto a greased tray and allow to cool.

Once cool blitz in robot coupe and spread dust like mixture onto a baking tray lined with slip mat or baking parchment.

Bake in hot oven until golden brown.

Remove from oven and cut out rounds with cutter and shape into small baskets.

Leave to cool.

For the cider brandy chantilly

Place cream and sugar in a bowl.

Whisk until whipped.

Stir in brandy.

To serve

Place crumble onto plate and remove ring.

Quenelle the cider cream onto plate.

Scoop sorbet into croquant baskets.

Garnish with some apple julienne and finish with apple crisp.

108
MILLER HOWE RESTAURANT AND HOTEL

Rayrigg Road, Windermere, Cumbria LA23 1EY

01539 442 536
www.millerhowe.com

Let me introduce you to one of the most hidden gems in the Lake District. This is a place where I am privileged to work and I am delighted to welcome you to stop by anytime you are passing to see for yourself what I am about to describe to you.

Step into the Miller Howe and be absolutely enamoured by the elegant interiors, open fires in the winter, and a warm and friendly welcome all year round. Explore our lounges, beautifully decorated with William Morris wallpaper, spot some of our arts and crafts pieces selected with care by present owners Martin and Helen Ainscough. Move through to the conservatory and be astounded by the views of Lake Windermere and the fells beyond. If you can tear yourself away, let one of our team lead you to the restaurant, again with unsurpassed views, and let our head chef Andrew Beaton and his talented brigade of young chefs fill your tastebuds with food that is prepared to the highest quality. Andrew, who has been at the Miller Howe for three years, is a fast, up and coming competent chef who is starting to have his talent recognised at the highest level. He believes in sourcing all his products as locally as possible, and takes great pleasure in using Cumbria's fine and ever expanding choice of meat, game, fish and vegetables.

Andrew and his brigade will then bring together everything that's local, to produce simply cooked food with dense flavours. If you have a few days to spare or even just one night, why not come and stay with us. We have fifteen stylish bedrooms, some of which have views over Lake Windermere and the fells, all of which have modern facilities and offer you a comfortable nights sleep. After dinner, try a glass of our owners' personally selected house wines, or treat yourself to a bottle of something special from our considerable wine list. Why not relax in the comfort of our lounges and enjoy a nightcap before adjourning to bed. We also have a most beautifully located terrace. On a summers day there is nothing more pleasant than having a lazy lunch, or perhaps afternoon tea, with a Pimms or a glass of champagne. The terrace offers peace and tranquility, you may even catch a glimpse of our local wildlife that inhabits the gardens. Enjoy views that will stay with you for ever, making you want to return time after time to experience what the Miller Howe and its dedicated team have to offer.

Built as a private residence in 1916,
today Miller Howe offers comfortable
'arts and crafts' interiors, indulgent
cuisine and simply unforgettable views

SALMON ASSIETTE

SERVES 4

Ingredients

Rillette

1 salmon side skinned
250g butter
1 lemon
1 bunch chopped tarragon
75g chopped parsley
50g baby capers

Gravadlax

1 salmon side skinned
75g caster sugar
75g salt
8 juniper berries
2 lemons, grated rind

Smoked Salmon Terrine

1 side of smoked salmon
1 kilo tub of cream cheese
1 bunch chopped chives
pinch of paprika

Method

For the rillette

Melt the butter in a heavy bottomed saucepan, add salmon and return to heat, cook until salmon is lightly poached in the butter, remove from heat and cool down. Once cooled add chopped herbs, the juice of one lemon, baby capers and season with salt and pepper. Lay cling film out on a work top, place some of the salmon mixture on the cling film and roll into a cylindrical shape, refrigerate for 4 hours.

For the gravadlax

Mix all the salt, sugar, lemon rind and juniper berries together, pack the salt mixture around the salmon and tightly wrap in cling film, refrigerate for 6 hours then rinse thoroughly and place chopped dill on the top.

For the smoked salmon terrine

Line a terrine mould with cling film, put a layer of smoked salmon on the bottom. Mix the cream cheese, chives and paprika together, spread a thin layer of the mixture on the salmon, keep repeating the process until the mould is full. Refrigerate for 8 hours before you use it.

To serve

Assemble the dish as in the photograph.

CUMBRIAN PORK THREE WAYS

SERVES 4

Ingredients

1 pork fillet
1 pork belly
1 pigs cheek
1 savoy cabbage
250g split green peas
5 Granny Smith apples
4 slices of pancetta
4ltr duck fat
200ml apple juice
½ litre dark chicken stock
1 carrot
200g block pancetta
100g sugar
1 lemon

Method

Wrap the pork fillet in the slices of pancetta and wrap in cling film. Place the pork belly in the goose fat and cover with tin foil then cook at 90°C in the oven for 5 hours. Once cooked remove from fat and put on tray.

Chill it down then cut into oblong shapes as in picture, reheat as needed. Heat a frying pan and colour the pigs cheek until golden brown, add the apple juice and reduce by half, add the chicken stock, cover the pan with tin foil and place in the oven at 110c for 3 hours.

In a saucepan add the split green peas, carrot and pancetta block, cover with water, bring to the boil, and cook until peas are soft and are breaking up, drain any excess water off, season with salt and pepper.

Finely shred the savoy cabbage and cook in butter until soft, season with salt and pepper.

Peel the apples and place in a saucepan, cook down with the sugar and add the juice of one lemon. Once cooked add the apples to a jug blender and puree until smooth.

To cook the pork fillet poach for 8 minutes in water then colour in a frying pan in olive oil until golden brown.

To serve

Assemble the dish as the photograph.

CHOCOLATE AND STRAWBERRY

SERVES 10

Ingredients

Chocolate Parfait

15 egg yolks
200g icing sugar
500g dark chocolate
1 litre cream

Financier

750g sugar
680g egg whites
500g beurre noisette
90g flour
380g ground almonds
120g cocoa powder

Strawberry Sorbet

1kg strawberry punnet
300g sugar
350g water

Strawberry and Vanilla Delice

200g strawberry puree
200g whipped cream
3 sheets of gelatine soaked in water
50g sugar

200g milk
200g whipped cream
3 sheets of gelatine soaked in water
50g sugar
2 vanilla pods

Method

For the chocolate parfait

Make a sabayon with the eggs and sugar, melt the chocolate and add the sabayon, whip the cream and fold in the chocolate sabayon and set.

For the financier

Whip whites until soft peaks and slowly add sugar, like meringue. Put butter on the stove until brown, pour on whites, fold in flour, ground almonds and cocoa powder, bake at 180°C until knife comes out clean.

For the strawberry sorbet

Purée the strawberries and pass through a sieve, boil the sugar and water, simmer for 3 minutes, add syrup and purée together, cool then churn in an ice cream machine.

For the strawberry and vanilla delice

Boil up the purée and sugar, add the soaked gelatine, pass through a sieve, cool and fold together with the whipped cream. Set in a tray for 2 hours.

Boil the milk, sugar and vanilla pods, add the soaked gelatine, pass through a sieve, cool and add the whipped cream. Pour on top of the strawberry mousse and set for 2 hours.

118
THE QUINCE AND MEDLAR

13 Castlegate, Cockermouth, Cumbria CA13 9EU

01900 823 579
www.quinceandmedlar.co.uk

Twenty-five years ago if you suggested going to a vegetarian restaurant for an evening to your friends, they would probably have laughed, with thoughts of scrubbed pine tables, hard seats, piles of pulses and loads of lentils going through their minds. Well this is what Colin and Louisa Le Voi thought when they were invited to dine at Quince and Medlar in the small attractive Georgian market town of Cockermouth over twenty two years ago. What they experienced was so different from what they expected. They liked it so much they decided to buy the restaurant. The then owners had heard that Colin and Louisa were looking to set up a restaurant of their own but were committed to completing the season at Sharrow Bay Hotel on Lake Ullswater, where they both worked for the late Francis Coulson and Brian Sack. Colin training in the kitchen, and Louisa front of house. After finishing their shift late one spring night at Sharrow back in '88 there was a phone call from the owner of Quince and Medlar saying he had heard on the grapevine that they were on the lookout for a property to transform into a restaurant. Would they be interested in viewing Q & M as it was on the market. After a behind the scene and an upstairs tour, where the living quarters were, they fell in love with it straight away and said yes. The following year they moved in. Having both been born and raised in West Cumbria a deep fondness of the area had developed over the years and the listed Georgian town house next to the castle was the ideal position to start their own restaurant business. With nearly twenty two years behind them, the restaurant has seen many changes.

Their three children have been born into the 'foodie' world, an expansion into the adjoining property and numerous awards along the way, Colin and Louisa are very much dedicated to the restaurant serving beautifully imaginative vegetarian dishes that delight all good food lovers. Their use of fine seasonal crops and often vegetables from the organic garden, complement the comprehensive organic wine list and unusual fruit nectars. Dishes are prepared with artistic flair and style by Colin and Louisa, Louisa being the chief pudding maker who then goes forward to the dining room at night, which has a cosy, intimate, romantic feel. The sitting room with warm, red wine coloured walls and comfy armchairs is packed with character and charm. There are interesting paintings by respected Cumbrian artists. All the ingredients for a relaxing, vegetarian fine dining experience where even non-vegetarians certainly won't miss the meat.

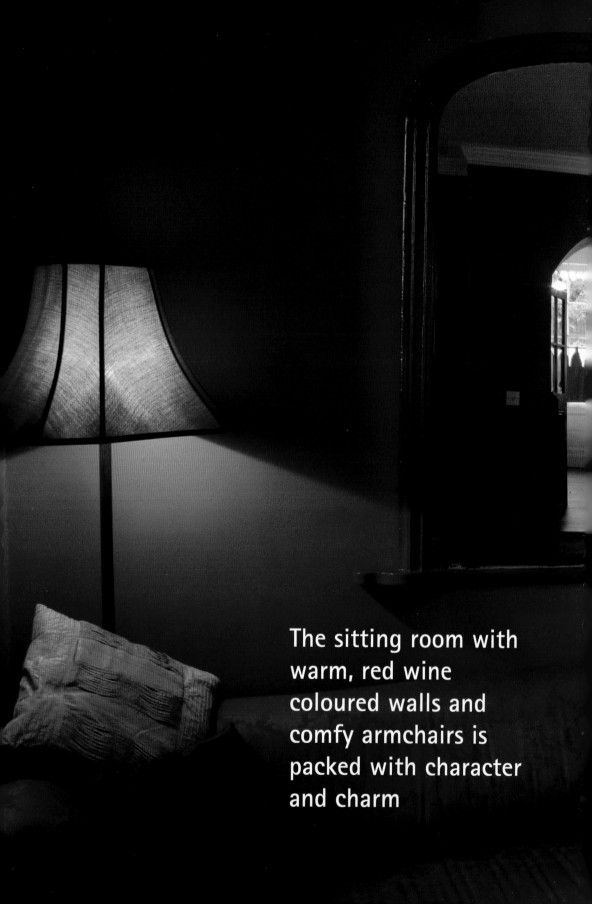

The sitting room with warm, red wine coloured walls and comfy armchairs is packed with character and charm

POTATO ROSTI ON WILTED SPINACH LEAVES WITH PAN FRIED QUAIL EGG AND MUSTARD SAUCE

SERVES 4

Method

Fry the onion and garlic lightly in a little oil.

While the onion is sweating, grate the potatoes.

Mix the onion, garlic, grated potato, parsley and seasoning together and form into 4 round discs (about 5cm in diameter).

Fry the discs until cooked through and golden brown on both sides.

Blanch the spinach leaves for 1 minute in boiling water and drain.

Fry the quail eggs.

Place spinach on a warmed plate, top with the potato, then fried quail egg.

Spoon the mustard sauce around and serve immediately.

For the mustard sauce

Mix all ingredients together and heat gently in a small pan.

Ingredients

4 small potatoes, grated
1 small onion, chopped
125g spinach leaves
1 clove garlic, crushed
splash olive oil
1tsp parsley chopped
salt and pepper
4 free range quail eggs

Mustard Sauce

1tsp Dijon mustard
1tsp balsamic vinegar
2tsp white wine
pinch turmeric
salt and pepper
100ml whipping cream

THORNBY MOOR SMOKED CUMBERLAND CHEESE SOUFFLÉ WRAPPED IN STRIPS OF COURGETTE ON A CHAR GRILLED MUSHROOM AND BAKED SWEET POTATO WITH A POMEGRANATE REDUCTION

SERVES 4

Ingredients

42g butter
42g unbleached white flour
275ml milk
2 medium free range eggs separated and 1 yolk
125g grated Cumberland smoked cheese
salt, pepper, nutmeg, cayenne pepper
2 medium courgettes thinly sliced lengthways
1 small sweet potato, sliced, seasoned and
baked for 10 minutes in a med/hot oven.
4 large mushrooms, stalks removed, grilled for
3-4 minutes under a hot grill
4tsp crème fraiche
pinch smoked paprika

Pomegranate and Red Wine Reduction

57g butter
1 shallot chopped
2tbsp balsamic vinegar
1 pomegranate seeded
200ml red wine
1tbsp chopped parsley

Method

Pre heat oven to gas mark 5, 190°C, 375°F

For the soufflé

Melt butter in a pan.

Stir in the flour, cook, then gradually add milk, cooking and stirring all the time over a medium heat until thickened.

Cool slightly.

Add cheese and seasoning.

Whisk egg whites with a pinch of salt until stiff.

Beat the egg yolks into the sauce, and then fold in the egg whites.

Spoon the mixture into 4 buttered ramekins, and sit these in a high sided baking tray.

Half fill the tray with water and put in the pre heated oven.

Bake until firm to the touch. 20 - 25 minutes.

Remove from the oven, take out of the ramekins when cool.

Turn up the oven to gas mark 6, 200°C, 400°F.

Place the slices of sweet potato inside the mushrooms, and then sit the soufflé on top.

Wrap the sliced courgette around the soufflé and mushroom and top with a dollop of crème fraiche and a sprinkling of grated smoked cheese and smoked paprika or cayenne pepper.

Bake in the oven for 20 minutes .

For the pomegranate reduction

Sweat shallots in butter for 2 minutes.

Add all other ingredients and simmer until reduced by one third.

Liquidise and pass through a sieve, serve.

CRUNCHIE CHOCOLATE TORTE

SERVES 4

Ingredients

250g good quality dark chocolate
45ml liquid glucose
40g caster sugar
1 orange, grated and juiced
4 tbsp strong black coffee
200ml whipping cream
cinder toffee*

Method

Line the bottom of 4 ramekins with greaseproof paper.

Gently melt all (except the cream and toffee) ingredients together in a bowl over a pan of boiling water.

Leave to cool for about an hour.

Crush the cinder toffee into small chunks.

Whip the cream until it forms soft peaks.

Fold together the cream, chocolate and cinder toffee.

Spoon into the ramekins and chill for several hours.

When ready to serve, cut around the edge of the ramekin with a knife, tip onto your hand, remove the lining paper and place onto the plate. Delicious with crème fraiche, cream or ice cream.

*Cinder toffee (use about ½ of this recipe for the chocolate torte, the rest can be saved in an airtight container for another occasion).

100g golden syrup

200g caster sugar

40g butter

1/2 tsp vinegar

1 tsp bicarbonate of soda

2 tbsp water

Line a 15cm square tin with greaseproof or parchment paper.

Put the syrup, sugar, butter and water into a large heavy - bottomed pan set over a medium heat. Stir until the sugar has dissolved, before turning up the heat and bringing to the boil.

Cook, without stirring until a teaspoon of the hot toffee mixture becomes a hard ball when dropped into a jug of cold water. If you have a sugar thermometer, it should register 138°C. Remove the pan from the heat.

Add the vinegar and bicarbonate of soda to the pan - take care as the toffee mixture will bubble up and rise in the pan. Pour immediately into the lined tin and leave on one side.

After about 15 - 20 minutes, when the mixture has begun to set, score the toffee in square shapes, using a sharp knife. Break along the lines when it has completely set. The toffee will keep in an airtight tin for up to 2 weeks.

128
RAMPSBECK COUNTRY HOUSE HOTEL

Watermillock, Ullswater, Cumbria CA11 OLP

01768 486 442
www.rampsbeck.co.uk

Revealing "The Lake District's best kept secret".

Nestled on the foreshore of Ullswater is Rampsbeck Country House Hotel, an AA three red star property. Its natural parklands and manicured gardens make for a spectacular setting for this Three Rosette awarded Restaurant. Privately owned, the hotel has seen major investment and refurbishment over the past two years.

Head Chef Andrew McGeorge, who has been with the hotel for over 20 years, together with his team offer an array of traditional French and British cuisine presented in a modern way.

Mainly locally sourced ingredients are used within the ever evolving menu including Herdwick lamb from Yew Tree Farm, Lowther Estate venison from Cartmel game, and cheeses from the Winter Farm Shop, as well as wild sea bass from the Solway Firth.

Further afield lobsters are sourced from Morecambe bay. Fresh fruit and vegetables are provided by James' of Penrith.

The relaxed, yet sophisticated approach to service provides the perfect ambience to complement the quality of food.

Guests can also enjoy an interesting selection of old and new world wines with over 200 bins on offer.

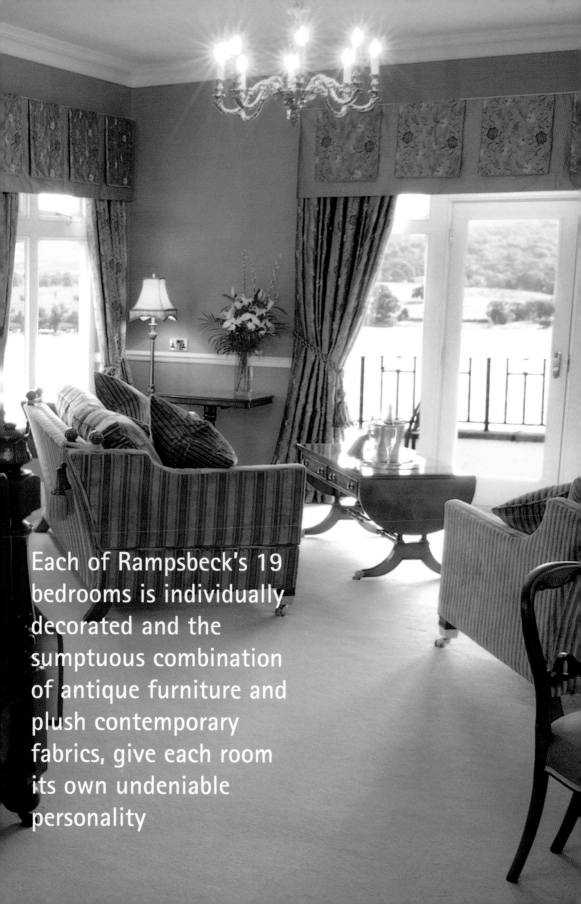

Each of Rampsbeck's 19 bedrooms is individually decorated and the sumptuous combination of antique furniture and plush contemporary fabrics, give each room its own undeniable personality

TRONCHON OF FOIE GRAS WITH ORANGE DRESSING AND PAIN D'ÉPICE CRUMBLE

SERVES 4

Ingredients

Tronchon

500g foie gras
ground white pepper
salt

Orange Dressing

4 oranges
100ml white wine vinegar
1 shallot
100ml truffle oil
100ml extra virgin olive oil

Pain d'épice Crumble

100g soft flour
100g caster sugar
100g butter
1tsp ground cinnamon
1tsp ground ginger
grated zest ½ lemon
grated zest ½ orange

Method

For the tronchon of foie gras

Clean Foie Gras, remove skin and veins. Break into small pieces, add seasonings, roll up tight into cling film then tin foil into a cylinder shape, chill for 2 hours then place in water for 15 minutes, chill again.

For the orange dressing

Segment 1 orange – keep for garnish. Peel 3 oranges and cut into quarters, squeeze juice, place into a pan with the shallot and white wine vinegar, heat slowly, reduce by half, liquidise and pass through fine chinois, whisk in truffle and olive oil, then season.

For the pain d'épice crumble

Rub in butter with the dry ingredients, place onto a greased metal tray, bake in oven for 20 minutes, when golden brown, remove from oven. Cool, then break into small pieces.

PAN FRIED BEST END AND BRAISED LEG OF YEW TREE FARM, HERDWICK LAMB WITH WILTED WILD GARLIC, ROASTED BANANA SHALLOT, ROSEMARY JUS AND CHERRY VINE TOMATOES

SERVES 4

Ingredients

1kg leg of lamb
500g best end of lamb
200g wild garlic
4 banana shallots
20 cherry vine tomatoes
1 bunch rosemary
1 tbspn tomato purée
3 cloves garlic
300g mire poix
3 onions
3 carrots
1 leek
½ head of celery
½ bottle red wine

Method

For the braised Leg

Season lamb, add crushed garlic and ½ bunch of rosemary. Tie up, seal until brown in hot fat, add mire poix, sweat off, add tomato puree and red wine, add water to cover meat. Place tin foil over tin and braise for 4 hours. Cool slightly, breakdown the meat, season and roll up into a cylinder shape, chill. Slice into 8, then coat in bread crumbs and chill, when required deep fry until golden brown. The braising liquor pass through a fine chinoise and reduce with rosemary until correct consistency.

For the best end of lamb

Season the best end, in a hot pan with little oil, seal on both sides for 2 minutes then rest and slice when required.

For the roasted banana shallot

Peel shallot, seal in hot fat and season, place in oven for 8 minutes.

For the cherry vine tomatoes

Coat with olive oil and sea salt, place under hot grill until soft.

To serve

As in picture.

CHOCOLATE AND RASPBERRY MOUSSE, RASPBERRY SORBET AND JELLY

SERVES 4

Ingredients

125g extra bitter chocolate 70%
100g raspberry purée
200g lightly whipped cream
Brilliance Noire – chocolate glaze
625g of raspberries
300ml stock syrup
1 sheet gold leaf
2½ leaves gelatine

Method

For the chocolate and raspberry mousse

Melt chocolate add the warm raspberry purée and fold in the lightly whipped cream. Pour into mould and chill for 2 hours. Melt the glaze and pour onto the chocolate mousse.

For the raspberry sorbet

In a liquidiser put 200ml of stock syrup and 375g of raspberries. When puréed, pass and place into a sorbet machine or freezer.

For the raspberry jelly

Place 250g of raspberries and 100ml of stock syrup over a bain marie for 1 hour. Pass raspberry juice, add melted gelatine leaves and place into a small container and chill for 2 hours.

138
ROTHAY MANOR HOTEL

Ambleside, Cumbria LA22 0EH

01539 433 605
www.rothaymanor.co.uk

Rothay Manor Hotel & Restaurant is situated in the heart of the Lake District, just a short walk from the centre of Ambleside. Set in its own landscaped gardens, the house was originally built in 1823 as a summer residence for a Liverpool shipping merchant and has been owned and personally managed by the Nixon family since 1967.

From its origins as a "tiny hotel with first class restaurant", the hotel has grown a little, but the restaurant still retains the excellent reputation for first class cuisine, wine and service combined with a comfortable, relaxed and friendly atmosphere.

Head Chef, Jane Binns, has been at the hotel for over 30 years and, together with her team, offers delicious seasonal menus with all dishes freshly prepared using local produce from the surrounding lakes and fells wherever possible, as well as from the nearby west coast.

The restaurant is light and airy with views over the garden, and well-spaced tables laid in a classical style with fine china, silver and crystal allowing for "intimate" dining. Catering for a maximum of forty diners, there is also a private function room that can accommodate up to thirty four diners.

Consistently listed in the Good Food Guide for forty one years, Rothay Manor was a finalist in the Cumbria Tourism "Taste" Awards in 2008 and, more recently, shortlisted for "Small Hotel of the Year" and "Access for All" in the Cumbria Tourism Awards for 2010.

From its origins as a "tiny hotel with first class restaurant", the hotel has grown a little, but the restaurant still retains the excellent reputation for first class cuisine, wine and service combined with a comfortable, relaxed and friendly atmosphere

ROAST QUAIL WITH CHICKEN LIVER PATÉ
SERVES 4

Ingredients

2 roast quail
16 grapes
4 circles white bread
225g diced pancetta
55g butter large pinch of thyme

Paté

120g butter
¼ pint whipping cream
230g chicken livers
25ml brandy
1 tsp mixed oregano and thyme

Sauce

glass of white wine
1 onion
1 carrot
1 chicken stock cube
¼ pint whipping cream

Method

For the quail

Season quail and roast for 45 minutes at 200°C. Joint when cooked.

Make stock with bones, chopped onion, carrot, chicken stock cube and white wine. Reduce and thicken slightly with cornflour. Add the cream and reduce again until it covers the back of a spoon.

For the paté

Sauté chicken livers with herbs, butter, brandy and cream and bring to the boil. Blend till smooth.

Dice pancetta and fry until crispy.

Fry bread circles in butter, sunflower oil and thyme until crisp.

To serve

Spread paté on bread circles and top each with a leg and a breast of quail. Garnish plate with grapes and pancetta and drizzle sauce over the quail.

SEA BASS WITH SPINACH LEAVES AND MUSHROOMS

SERVES 4

Ingredients

4 x 170g sea bass fillets
(ask fishmonger for bones)
250g bag baby spinach leaves
3 large banana shallots
1 onion
1 leek
1 carrot
2 bay leaves
170g assorted wild mushrooms
120g butter
1 glass dry white wine
1 tbsp chopped coriander
black peppercorns
½ pint whipping cream
lemon juice
salt and pepper
fresh parsley
water

Purée

3/4lb parsnips
55g butter

Method

For the sauce

Brown fish bones in a hot oven for 10 minutes. Put in a pan with chopped onion, carrot, bay leaves, white wine, black peppercorns, a dash of lemon juice. Add enough water to cover, bring to the boil and simmer for ½ hour. Strain and thicken slightly with cornflour. Add ½ pint whipping cream and reduce until it covers the back of a spoon.

For the fricasse

Sauté shallots. Add chopped wild mushrooms and white wine. Reduce until wine is absorbed. Fold in chopped coriander.

For the parsnip purée

Peel and trim parsnips, reserve one parsnip for parsnip crisps and boil the rest in salted water until soft. Mash with 60g butter, salt and pepper until smooth.

For the parsnip crisps

Peel the trimmed parsnip thinly lengthways and fry in a deep fat fryer until golden brown.

Lightly sauté spinach leaves in butter and season.

Season sea bass fillets, brush top with butter and grill.

To serve

Place sea bass fillets on a base of spinach leaves, with the mushroom fricassee around the outside.

Place a quenelle of parsnip purée on top of the sea bass and drizzle sauce over the top.

Decorate with parsnip crisps and fresh parsley.

CHOCOLATE AND DAMSON PARFAIT

SERVES 10

Ingredients

For The Parfait

80g egg yolks (approx 2 eggs)
50g water
130g sugar
250g damson puree
250g white chocolate
250g double cream
250g dark chocolate
10 6.5cm x 4cm rings

For The Damson Gin Coulis

110g damsons
110g sugar
2 tbsp gin

For The Truffle

100g dark chocolate
200g semi-whipped cream

Method

For the parfait

Place rings in the freezer.

Boil the water and sugar until it 'threads'.

Add the mixture to the egg yolks and mix gently.

Whip the double cream and add the yolk mix.

Fold in the damson purée.

Repeat the above replacing the damson purée with white chocolate and dark chocolate.

Taking 1 ring at a time from the freezer. Place dark chocolate parfait at the bottom, followed by damson parfait and topped by white chocolate parfait and return to the freezer quickly to set for 1 hour.

Remove from the freezer and turn out onto a plate. Place a quenelle of the chocolate truffle on the top of the parfait and drizzle the coulis over and around the dessert.

Garnish with chocolate shavings.

For the damson gin coulis

Boil the damsons and sugar and add gin to flavour and strain.

For the chocolate truffle

Melt the chocolate and add to the cream. Leave to set.

148
THE SAMLING

Ambleside Road, Windermere, Cumbria LA23 1LR

01539 431 922
www.thesamlinghotel.co.uk

Nigel Mendham's restaurant at The Samling is the regions latest to be awarded the highly coveted Michelin star. The three AA rosette restaurant offers guests some of the finest modern British cuisine that you will find anywhere. Nigel balances classical flavours meticulously prepared with a contemporary flair to produce both stunning presentation and taste; this is an idiosyncratic balance that works in perfect harmony.

The hotel has eleven beautifully appointed bedrooms which give the guests of the restaurant the opportunity to stay over and enjoy The Samling's extensive wine list or Nigel's famous Gourmand 7- course Tasting Menu which includes a selection of wines which perfectly match Nigel's superb cuisine.

The hugely popular hotel's restaurant has stunning elevated views of lake Windermere. When combined with discreet service that is so effortless you will hardly notice it, it's easy to see why The Samling hotel is rapidly becoming one of the most popular intimate foodie hotspots of the North.

The three AA rosette restaurant offers guests some of the finest modern British cuisine that you will find anywhere

RED MULLET, PARMESAN CUSTARD, TOMATO MARMALADE

SERVES 4

Ingredients

Red Mullet

450g red mullet scaled, filleted and pin boned

Tomato Marmalade

55g diced red onion
15g water
7g red wine vinegar
20g caster sugar
400g tomatoes diced
1 clove garlic purée
2 tsp tomato ketchup

Parmesan Custard

1/3 cup double cream
1/3 cup milk
85g grated parmesan
1 egg
2 egg yolk

Parmesan Foam

200ml milk
100g grated parmesan
25g cold diced butter
salt

Method

For the tomato marmalade

Sweat shallot, onion, water and garlic.

Add vinegar and sugar.

Add the tomatoes.

Cook until all the liquid has evaporated.

Season to taste.

For the parmesan custard

Simmer the cream, milk and parmesan.

Infuse for 30 minutes.

Whisk together the eggs and yolks.

Reheat the cheese mixture.

Sieve the cream onto the eggs.

Season to taste.

Cook at 120ºC for 30 minutes.

For the parmesan foam

Warm the milk and butter.

Add the parmesan.

Allow to infuse.

Season to taste.

To garnish

1 courgette.

Aged balsamic vinegar.

HERDWICK MUTTON 'ALL THINGS SCOTCH'

SERVES 4

Ingredients

Mutton

1 loin mutton
1 Warrior haggis
25ml whisky
1 shoulder mutton flat boned
½ bottle white wine
white peppercorns
bay leaf
salt

Vegetables

100g pearl barley
1 swede
2 carrots
½ celeriac
2 turnips
2 shallots
sprig thyme
500g curly kale
100g button onions
25g cold diced butter

Method

For the mutton

Place the mutton shoulder into a tray lined with baking parchment.

Add white wine and the same amount of water.

Add a few peppercorns and bay leaf.

Season.

Cover with baking parchment and tin foil.

Cook for 8 hours at 110°C.

Simmer haggis in water for 40 minutes.

Take out, remove skin and drizzle over whisky.

Set to one side.

When cool make haggis quenelles.

Coat the haggis in flour, then milk, then flour again.

Cook when needed at 180°C for 3 - 4 minutes.

Remove mutton shoulder from the oven.

Sieve the cooking liquor into a pan and reduce until sticky.

Fold into picked shoulder meat, season.

Vac pack tightly and roll out.

For the vegetables

Rinse pearl barley under cold water.

Cook till soft.

Brunoise all root vegetables.

Dice shallot.

Pick thyme leaves.

Sweat shallot until soft with no colour.

Add root vegetables and thyme.

Cook till soft.

Add pearl barley, season, add diced butter, mix until butter has emulsified.

CHOCOLATE PEANUT CRUNCH

SERVES 4

Ingredients

Chocolate Fondant

125g butter
125g dark chocolate
3 egg yolks
3 whole eggs
60g sugar
25g flour

Peanut Crunch

25g dark chocolate
30g cocoa butter
115g peanut butter
30g chopped peanuts
55g feuilletine

Peanut Bomb

2 eggs
45g icing sugar
120g double cream
2 leaves gelatine
110g smooth peanut butter

Method

For the fondant

Melt together butter and chocolate.

Whisk eggs and yolks until tripled in volume.

Slowly add sugar.

Continue to whisk.

Slowly add melted chocolate mixture.

Gently fold in flour.

For the peanut crunch

Melt chocolate and butter.

Beat peanut butter until creamy.

Add a pinch of salt.

Add chopped nuts.

Add melted chocolate mixture.

Add feuilletine.

Roll out thinly between baking paper.

Freeze.

For the bomb

Whisk eggs and icing together, continue whisking over a bain marie.

Beat peanut butter until creamy.

Boil double cream, add soaked gelatine.

Slowly add cream to peanut butter whisking all the time.

Fold in sabayon and set in moulds.

To serve

Cut out peanut crunch the same size as the base of the bomb.

Put a bomb onto each peanut crunch.

Place back in the freezer until ready to serve.

Cook the chocolate fondant for 4 - 5 minutes at 180°C.

Take out the peanut crunch to soften slightly.

Caramelise 3 slices of banana.

Garnish with chocolate tuille and chocolate sauce.

158
SHARROW BAY COUNTRY HOUSE HOTEL

Lake Ullswater, Penrith, Cumbria CA10 2LZ

01768 486 301
www.sharrowbay.co.uk

The restaurant at Sharrow Bay is internationally renowned. The hotel has achieved a Michelin star for the past 15 consecutive years and when combined with a beautiful lakeside setting and one of the best wine lists in the world it is easy to see why Sharrow Bay is one of the most critically acclaimed restaurants in the country.

Head Chefs Colin Akrigg and Mark Teasdale were both born on nearby farms almost within site of the hotels kitchens and these local roots are clearly evident in Sharrow Bay menus. Long before it was fashionable to do so, the head chefs insisted on sourcing their ingredients for the renowned Sharrow kitchens locally. This includes delicious venison from the neighbouring valley of Martindale and sumptuous lamb from Yew Tree Farm at Coniston.

The restaurant at Sharrow has always been pioneering and helping shape what we now know as modern British cuisine. Indeed in the 1970's the Sharrow kitchen was the birthplace of the famous British dish sticky toffee pudding. More recently the Sharrow Bay food experience hasn't been limited to the Sharrow kitchens with the annual takeover of the Harvey Nichols restaurant becoming a hugely popular and sort after experience. To mark the hotel's 60th anniversary the hotel even launched a new locally sourced food range including soups, casseroles and desserts into the likes of Booths, Waitrose, Lakeland and Ocado.

The restaurant at Sharrow has always been pioneering helping shape what we now know as modern British cuisine. Indeed in the 1970's the Sharrow kitchen was the birthplace of the famous British dish sticky toffee pudding

WARM SALAD OF SQUAB PIGEON WITH ROASTED FIGS

SERVES 4

Ingredients

1 whole pigeon
selection of salad leaves including
frizzie endive, lollo rosso, micro red
chard, pea shoots

Dressing

1 shallot
1 small garlic clove
½ tsp sugar
3 parts flavourless oil
1 part white wine vinegar
1 tsp English mustard

Roasted Figs

8 figs
25g butter
¼ bottle of port
2 tbsp runny honey

Pancetta

2 pieces of pancetta

Method

For the pigeon

Season the pigeon with salt and pepper.

Seal the pigeon in a hot pan until golden brown, roast in an oven at 200ºC for 15 minutes then allow to rest for 10 minutes.

When ready to serve warm through, take off the bone and serve with dressed leaves, roasted figs, crisp pancetta and a little juice from the figs.

Clean the mixed salad leaves and keep to one side.

For the dressing

Chop 1 shallot, 1 small garlic clove, ½ teaspoon salt, ½ teaspoon sugar and mix together in a bowl with 3 parts flavourless oil, 1 part white wine vinegar and 1 teaspoon English mustard. Mix all ingredients together and keep to one side.

For the figs

Roast the figs.

Butter the figs with a brush and lightly dust with caster sugar, honey and port.

Roast in a tray covered in foil until heated through for about 20 minutes at 200ºC.

Leave to cool in the liquid.

For the pancetta

Lie the pancetta between 2 sheets of parchment and press between 2 flat trays.

Bake in oven at 200ºC for 7 – 10 minutes until golden allow to cool and crisp up.

TENDERLOIN AND CONFIT BELLY OF CUMBERLAND PORK WITH BLACK PUDDING AND APPLE AND SAGE SAUCE

SERVES 4

Ingredients

450g belly pork
1 tbsp sea salt
10 peppercorns
4 streaks of lemon zest
4 sprigs of rosemary
2 tbsp of oil
duck fat to cover

Black Pudding

5kg dried pigs blood
1 onion (finely chopped)
230g caster sugar
450g sultanas
½ pint champagne vinegar
sprig of rosemary and thyme
4 bay leaves
1kg lamb sweetbreads
230g pork fat

Apple and Sage Sauce

2 shallots chopped
4 sprigs of finely chopped sage
2 tbsp runny honey
1 Granny Smith apple chopped
1 pint demi glaze
1pint chicken stock
2 tbsp cider vinegar

Tenderloin of Pork

1 pork tenderloin (whole), fully seasoned
200g pancetta

Cabbage

1 savoy cabbage
1 carrot
¼ celeriac chopped to a fine brunoise
1 onion (chopped)
3 tbsp double cream

Method

For the belly pork

Marinade overnight with 1 tbsp of sea salt, 10 peppercorns, 4 streaks of lemon zest, 4 sprigs rosemary, 2 tbsp oil.

The next day cook at 90ºC, submerged in duck fat for one day or until tender – remove from fat and press between cling film and two trays weighted down.

For the black pudding

Cook together the following ingredients for approximately five minutes or until golden and syrupy. 5kg of dried pigs blood, 1 onion finely chopped, 230g caster sugar, 450g of sultanas, ½ pint champagne vinegar, sprig of rosemary and thyme, 4 bay leaves, 1kg lamb sweetbreads, 230g pork fat.

Mix the pigs blood with warm water until it resembles a consistency of ketchup. Combine with the ingredients above.

Mix well together and roll in cling film and poach for 25 minutes.

For the apple and sage sauce

Brown the shallots and apples in a sauce pan. Add sage stalks and vinegar and reduce. Add honey, demi glaze and chicken stock and reduce to your desired consistency and season to taste.

For the tenderloin of pork

Wrap the tenderloin of pork in pancetta, lightly season and roast on a rack for 7 minutes on each side and at a temperature of 200 ºC.

For the cabbage

Take apart the cabbage leaves and blanch for 3 minutes and refresh in iced water, small amounts at a time – finely slice. Sweat the brunoise onto the cabbage, season and heat through with cream.

To serve

Assemble dish on plate and pour round the sauce.

RHUBARB JELLY, ORANGE POLENTA CAKE AND A GINGER MASCARPONE

SERVES 4

Ingredients

Special Equipment

stencil
4 inch jelly moulds
6 inch square tin

Rhubarb Jelly

300g chopped rhubarb
200g caster sugar
75ml white wine
250ml water
4 leaves of gelatine/pint water
1 vanilla pod

Orange Polenta Cake

1 egg
50g soft butter
25g self raising flour
25g fine polenta
zest and juice of ½ an orange
25g caster sugar

Ginger Mascarpone

125g mascarpone
20g caster sugar
50ml stem ginger juice
1/2 leaf of gelatine
125ml double cream
1 stem ginger finely grated

Tuile

40g butter
50g icing sugar
1 egg white
40g plain flour

Candied Orange

1 orange
226g caster sugar
284ml water

Orange Sauce

4 oranges
56g caster sugar

Method

For the jelly (this can be prepared the day before)

Chop rhubarb into 3/4 inch pieces and put into a tray with sugar, water, white wine and one pod split in half lengthways, cover with foil and roast in the oven at 150°C for 25 minutes until tender then leave to cool. Strain the juice from the rhubarb and measure out the liquid.

For the cake

Cream butter and sugar until pale, add the egg and beat vigorously. Finally fold in the flour, polenta and zest.
Bake at 180°C in a 6 inch square cake tin, greased and lined, for approximately 20 minutes until risen and golden.
Make a syrup with orange juice and 40g sugar and brush onto the cooked cake. Cool and cut into 1/2 inch squares.

For the ginger mascarpone

Beat mascarpone and sugar until smooth. Warm ginger syrup and add gelatine (which has been softened in cold water) and one grated root of stem ginger. Add liquid to mascarpone and mix. Softly whip the cream and fold into the mixture, chill in the refrigerator.

For the tuile

Beat the egg whites and sugar until mixed together.
Add the melted butter to the mixture and fold in the flour.
Leave to rest in the fridge overnight.
Spread the mixture thinly onto baking parchment, and cut out using a plastic stencil in the shape of a cross.
Place cross onto a baking tray and cook at 150°C until golden in colour.
Spread the cross shape over the base of a pudding basin.
Carefully peel away from the basin and keep in an airtight container before use.

For the candied orange

Peel one orange with a potato peeler, and cut into thin juliennes.
Place in a pan of boiling water and strain.
Repeat this process 4 times to remove all bitterness from the orange julienne.
Place sugar in a saucepan and add water. Bring to the boil.
Add the orange julienne to the syrup and allow to boil for one minute.

For the orange sauce

Strain the juice of 4 oranges and add the sugar.
Bring the mixture to the boil and allow to reduce and then place in the fridge to chill.

To serve

See photograph.

168
THE SUN INN

6 Market Street Kirkby Lonsdale Cumbria LA6 2AU

01524 271 965
www.sun-inn.info

The 17th century Sun Inn in the heart of Kirkby Lonsdale overlooks St Mary's Church and is just a few steps from Ruskin's View; described by Ruskin as 'one of the fairest in England and therefore the World'.

The five star inn offers a luxury blend of old and new; real fires, beams, flagstone and oak floors combine comfortably with leather chairs, stylish restaurant and a modern kitchen.

Dining at the Sun Inn is relaxed and informal with caring service from a professional and friendly team including the owners Mark and Lucy Fuller and manager Steven Turner.

Sam Carter, Head Chef, has been at the Sun Inn for three years and has built up an excellent reputation and a number of awards and accolades. He manages a small team of talented chefs that prepare dishes with care, understanding and skill.

Fresh, Seasonal and Local; these three little words are our motto when planning menus at the Sun Inn. Fresh means our ingredients are delivered and prepared each day, seasonal ensures that the ingredients we choose are at their best, local is choosing the fabulous ingredients that are closest to home.

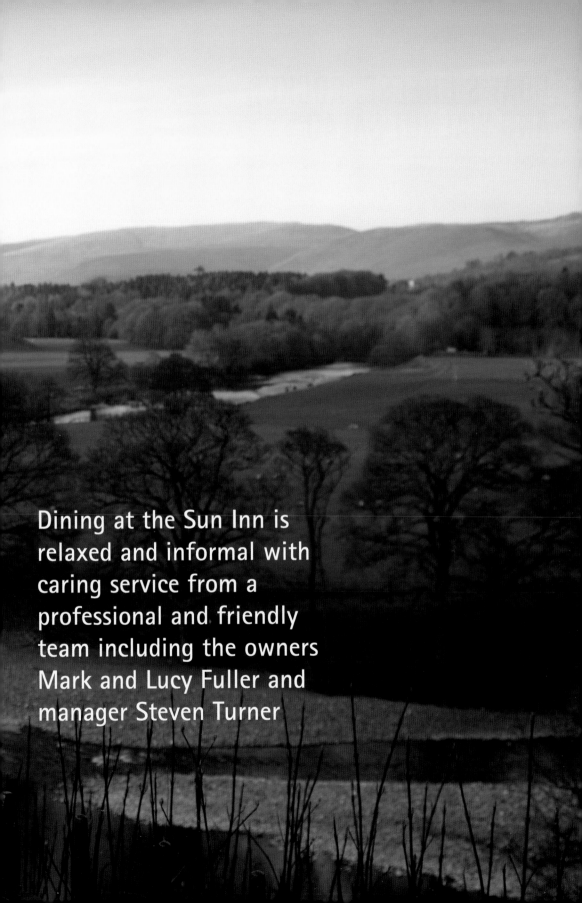

Dining at the Sun Inn is relaxed and informal with caring service from a professional and friendly team including the owners Mark and Lucy Fuller and manager Steven Turner

GOAT'S CHEESE, ROCKET AND WALNUT SALAD

SERVES 4 AS A STARTER

Method

Put the sugar and butter into a pan over a moderate heat, let it bubble up and swirl the pan to form a nice caramel. Carefully add the brandy (it will flame up so stand back), when the flames subside stir in the nuts and cook for approximately 5 minutes over a low heat until evenly coated in caramel. Leave to cool slightly, transfer to a food processor and blitz to a chunky purée. On a large work surface roll out cling film, then spread the walnut puree onto the cling film and place the goat's cheese log on top. Now roll the cling film up so that the goat's cheese is completely covered in the walnut puree. Tie the ends and place in the fridge to set.

Meanwhile, put the beetroot on a baking tray with plenty of rock salt, a good splash of balsamic vinegar and a drizzle of rapeseed oil. Place in a moderate oven and bake for approximately 20 minutes or until cooked, remove and leave to cool slightly before peeling and quartering.

Whisk up all the ingredients for the dressing and season to taste.

Slice the goat's cheese into 4 equal portions and grill briefly, to just warm the cheese and give a melting texture.

To serve

Coat the salad leaves in the dressing and place a small pile in the centre of each plate, with the apple slices. Dot the beetroot around and place the warmed goat's cheese on the top, finish with a drizzle of dressing and a few sprigs of red amaranth.

Ingredients

For The Cheese

250g goat's cheese log (rind removed)
125g shelled walnuts
1 tbsp muscavado sugar
10g unsalted butter
1 tbsp brandy

For The Dressing

1tsp Dijon mustard
1tsp honey
1 vanilla pod (split lengthways and seeds removed)
2 tbsp white wine vinegar
6 tbsp golden rapeseed oil

For The Salad

100g wild rocket salad leaves (picked and washed)
1 small head of frisee lettuce (picked and washed)
1 apple, (quartered, cored and sliced)
8 baby beetroot (trimmed of leaves but left unpeeled)
balsamic vinegar
golden rapeseed oil
rock salt
sprigs of red amaranth for garnish

BRAISED OXTAIL WITH MONKFISH, GLAZED ONIONS, CARROTS, TURNIPS AND CREAMED POTATO

SERVES 4

Ingredients

For The Oxtail

800g oxtail (cut into chunks)
1 small onion (chopped)
1 small carrot (chopped)
½ leek (chopped)
1 stick of celery (chopped)
2 cloves of garlic (chopped)
1 sprig fresh rosemary
1 small glass of red wine
400ml veal stock

Vegetables

8 baby turnips (leaves trimmed)
8 baby spring carrots (leaves trimmed)
8 silverskin onions (peeled)
1 tsp honey
100ml vegetable stock

For The Monkfish

4 x 100g portions monkfish
unsalted butter
golden rapeseed oil
creamy mashed potatoes
thyme for garnish

Method

For the oxtail

Season the oxtail. Add a splash of oil and a knob of butter to a frying pan and on a high heat seal on all sides until browned, transfer to a roasting dish. In the same pan sauté the vegetables for a few minutes, add the wine, then hot stock. Pour over the oxtail, cover and cook in a low oven for about 3 hours until the meat is tender and comes away from the bone easily. Leave to cool then carefully pick the meat from the bones, discarding them along with the vegetables. Put the meat to one side and strain the cooking liquid into a pan. On a moderate heat, reduce the liquid until it thickens slightly and becomes glossy, skimming off any fat that comes to the surface.

For the vegetables

Sauté the vegetables in a knob of butter, add the honey and enough vegetable stock to cover by half, season and stir. Cover with buttered paper and simmer gently for about 10 minutes, until cooked.

For the monkfish

Season the monkfish. Add a little rapeseed oil to a non-stick pan and seal over a high heat, add a knob of butter and when golden lower the heat and cook until firm but a little bouncy to touch.

To serve

Reheat the oxtail in the sauce and place in a small pile in the centre of the plates, sit the monkfish on top and dot the vegetables around, drizzle some of the sauce over and garnish with thyme. Serve with some creamy mashed potato on the side.

HOT CHOCOLATE AND CARAMEL FONDANT WITH HAZELNUT PRALINE AND DOUBLE JERSEY ICE CREAM

SERVES 4

Ingredients

For The Caramel

100g golden caster sugar
2tbsp honey
100ml double cream

For The Chocolate Sauce

45g dark chocolate (70% cocoa solids)
45ml full fat milk

For The Fondant

115g dark chocolate (70% cocoa solids)
115g unsalted butter
3 eggs
2 egg yolks
50g caster sugar
50g plain flour
4 fondant moulds
butter for greasing
cocoa powder for dusting

double jersey ice cream
hazelnut praline (roasted hazelnuts coated in caramelised sugar)

Method

For the caramel

Gently heat the sugar in a pan with a splash of water, swirl the pan and let it bubble up, cook until caramelised. In a separate pan heat up the cream and honey, add to the caramelised sugar. Simmer until slightly thickened and a golden toffee colour. Season with salt and pepper and freeze for at least 1 hour or until set.

For the fondants

Grease the inside of the moulds with butter and completely coat with cocoa powder to prevent the fondants from sticking.

Melt the chocolate and butter in a bowl over a simmering pan of water. In an electric mixer beat the eggs and sugar until tripled in volume. With the mixer on full speed add the melted chocolate and butter. Once incorporated fold in the flour and immediately pour ¾ of the mixture into the moulds. Put a dollop of caramel in the centre and then fill with the remaining fondant mixture. Cook on 200°C/180°C fan oven for about 10 minutes, until set around the edges but still soft and runny in the centre.

For the chocolate sauce

Heat the milk in a pan over a low heat, whisk in the chocolate until completely combined and smooth.

To serve

Put some chocolate sauce in the middle of each plate, put the fondant on top and carefully prise it from the mould (you may need to slide a thin knife around the edges to loosen it). Serve with double jersey ice cream and some chopped hazelnut praline.

178
THE SWAN HOTEL AND SPA

Newby Bridge, Cumbria LA12 8NB

01539 531 681
www.swanhotel.com

Situated at the southern tip of Lake Windermere, The Swan Hotel and Spa is very much a part of the local community and the fabric of the beautiful Lake District. This charming 17th century converted ale house has been lovingly restored following the disastrous floods of 2009. The devoted team has encapsulated country chic and it is perfect for a weekend away or dropping in for a spot of lunch by the riverside.

Food and wine lovers from miles around travel to enjoy the locally sourced, seasonal menu of the Swan Inn. Meals, hot chocolates and cask ales are served all day snuggled up by the fire side in the winter and riverside on the fabulous pink garden furniture in the summer. For those who want to get their glad rags on the River Room offers an extensive home cooked Italian themed menu using the finest local ingredients. The exceptional food is accompanied by a meticulously researched wine list bursting with rare vintages and is served by a team of knowledgeable and extremely vibrant staff.

There is never a dull moment at the Swan, the chic sophisticated décor is accompanied by a lively and bustling atmosphere, with an air of good fun and excitement. You will feel rejuvenated the second you walk through the door and may never want to leave.

The S

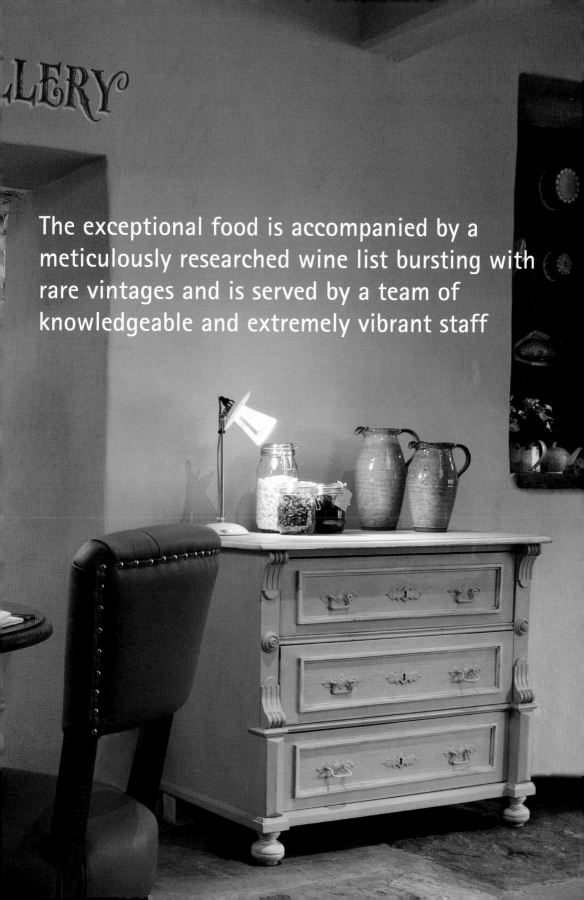

The exceptional food is accompanied by a meticulously researched wine list bursting with rare vintages and is served by a team of knowledgeable and extremely vibrant staff

DEEP FRIED GOOSNARGH DUCK EGG WITH ENGLISH ASPARAGUS AND MICRO HERBS

SERVES 4

Ingredients

4 duck eggs
20 aparagus tips
100g baby purple basil leaves
50g extra virgin olive oil
20g pine nuts
20g parmesan
4 handfuls of micro leaves
1 egg beaten
100g flour (seasoned)
100g breadcrumbs

Method

For the egg

Softly poach the duck eggs for approximately 90 seconds and immediately immerse in iced water to cool.

Coat the cooled, dry eggs in seasoned plain flour, beaten egg and breadcrumbs.

Deep fry the coated eggs until golden, place on top of the micro leaves and dress the plate with the basil pesto.

For the asparagus

Lightly blanch asparagus tips, immerse in iced water to chill and place on the plate.

For the pesto sauce

Prepare the pesto sauce by blending the basil leaves with the oil and add parmesan and pine nuts to taste.

Lightly dress a handful of micro leaves with a small amount of the pesto sauce and place on the asparagus.

PAN FRIED LINE CAUGHT SEA BASS WITH SAUTÉED POTATOES AND HERB SALAD

SERVES 4

Method

For the sea bass

Pan fry scaled, pin boned sea bass fillets skin side down for approx 2 minutes.

For the potatoes and spinach

Boil the potatoes, half and sauté them

Wilt the spinach in a pan with some butter.

To serve

Dress the plate with baby herbs, oil and balsamic vinegar.

Ingredients

20 new potatoes of equal size
8 handfuls of baby spinach leaves
4 sea bass fillets (pin boned)
drizzle of 15 year aged balsamic vinegar

CHOCOLATE, CARAMEL MOUSSE WITH SUMMER BERRIES

SERVES 4

Ingredients

4 sheets of acetate paper
250g chocolate
250g granulated sugar
150ml ice cold water
5 eggs
2 egg yolks
25g caster sugar
4 leaves of gelatine
300ml lightly whipped double cream

Method

For the chocolate

Make cone moulds out of pieces of acetate paper. To line the cones fill them with melted chocolate and pour out the excess. Allow to set until hard in the fridge.

For the caramel mousse

Heat 250g of granulated sugar in a thick bottomed saucepan until it is a dark caramel consistency.

Remove from the heat, carefully add 150ml of cold water and leave to cool.

While the caramel is cooling whisk 5 eggs and 2 egg yolks with 25g of caster sugar over a pan of boiling water. Once the eggs and sugar have formed a sabayon remove from the heat and whisk over iced water to cool.

Melt 4 leaves of pre soaked gelatine over a low heat and lightly whip 300ml of double cream in a separate bowl.

Combine the caramel, sabayon and gelatine then carefully fold in the cream.

Fill the cones with the mixture and place in the fridge to cool.

To serve

Serve with raspberry sorbet and summer berries.

188
WINDER HALL COUNTRY HOUSE HOTEL

Low Lorton, Cockermouth, Cumbria CA13 9UP

0190 085 107
www.winderhall.co.uk

Tucked away in the village of Lorton, Winder Hall is one of Cumbria's oldest and most historically important buildings. Not surprisingly, the Winders who set up home here in the 14th Century, chose beautiful, sheltered parkland at the northern end of the Buttermere valley to be at the centre of their royal estate. The house has changed and grown over the years but parts of the building still date back to Tudor times.

The dining room was formed out of the Jacobean hall, embellished and made more intimate with oak panelling dating from the Arts and Craft era. You would be forgiven for thinking this could lead to a formal and stuffy atmosphere but you would be wrong.

Ann and Nick Lawler who have owned Winder Hall since 2002 are not at all stuffy and their hospitality is genuinely relaxed and devoid of airs and graces. They somehow manage to juggle busy working lives with bringing up three children and a menagerie of animals (some of whom end up on the plate).

The prevailing attitude amongst their small team is that looking after people is the most important thing, being proud of the local produce and cooking really nice food is important as well, but dinner without fun is like alcohol-free wine; completely pointless.

The prevailing attitude
amongst their small
team is that looking
after people is the most
important thing, being
proud of the local
produce and cooking
really nice food is
important as well

NICK'S TOMATO AND RICOTTA SALAD WITH ANCHOVY TOAST

SERVES 6

Ingredients

selection of seasonal vine-ripened tomatoes
tin of anchovies
olive oil
white baguette
basil for garnish
ricotta cheese
salt and pepper for seasoning

Method

This is a really simple, refreshing and summery starter which takes no more than 10 minutes to knock-up. I love it for the taste and the presentation. It's a great start to a dinner party.

The flavour of your tomatoes is what sets this dish apart and I always like to have a selection of two or three to add interest and flavour to the plate.

To make the anchovy toast, whizz your anchovies in a processor and add a drop of olive oil to make sure you can drizzle some on the plate. Brush your thinly sliced baguette with the anchovy mixture and bake in the oven until the baguette is golden brown.

Place your toast, thinly-sliced tomato, ricotta (or a mild goat's cheese works well) on the plate, season your tomatoes with salt and pepper, drizzle some of the spare anchovy oil on the plate and finish with a basil garnish. Simple!

HELEN'S DUCK BREAST WITH MARMALADE AND PORT REDUCTION

SERVES 4

Ingredients

4 duck breasts
dash of olive oil for pan
small glass port
serving spoon seville marmalade
chicken stock
110g butter

Method

Score the duck breast season and place in a hot dry pan skin down, this helps to crisp the fat of the duck breast.

Cook for approx 7 mins or until the skin is golden brown.

Turn and cook for a further 5 mins.

Transfer on to a tray and place in a hot oven for a further 8 mins.

Drain off the fat from the pan and place back on the heat, until the pan nearly smokes.

Add the glass of port and flambé.

As the flames reduce add good quality marmalade. Here at Winder Hall we make our own in January, using good quality sevile oranges.

Add a quarter of a pint of chicken stock and 110g of butter. The reduction will thicken as it cooks.

Take the duck breast out and allow to rest.

Slice and place on sautéed potatoes and decorate with a vegetable garnish.

CLODAGH'S BAKEWELL TART
SERVES 10 - 12

Ingredients

Pastry

240g plain flour
140g diced cold butter
40g icing sugar
1 egg yolk to bind (add drop ice cold water
if necessary

Filling

200g each butter, castor sugar, ground almonds.
2 eggs, beaten
1 small tsp almond essence
raspberry or strawberry jam

Method

Pulse flour, butter and icing sugar in food processor until resembles breadcrumbs.

Add egg yolk to bind, plus water if necessary.

Chill in fridge for ½ hour and then roll out to line 10 - 12 inch loose bottomed flan tin.

Cover with layer of jam.

Meanwhile, heat butter for filling until just melted, then add sugar and cook for 1 min.

Then add eggs, ground almonds and almond essence.

Pour filling on top of jam layer, sprinkle with flaked almonds and bake for about 30 mins in hot oven (200°C, Gas 6) until risen and golden brown.

Filling should spring back into shape when lightly pressed with a finger.

RELISH CUMBRIA LARDER

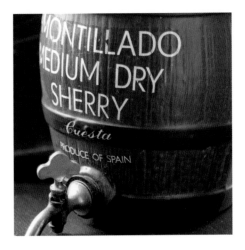

KESWICK BREWING COMPANY
The Old Brewery, Brewery Lane, Keswick CA12 5BY.
01768 780700,
www.keswickbrewery.co.uk
Cask real ale and bottled beers for sale on the site of the Old Allinsons Brewery.

STRAWBERRY BANK LIQUEURS
Wood Yeat Barn, Crossthwaite, Kendal LA8 8HX.
01539 568812,
www.strawberrybankliqueurs.co.uk
Damson beer and damson gin from fruit grown in orchards along the Lyth Valley.

ULVERSTON BREWING CO.
Diamond Buildings, Pennington Lane, Lindal-in-Furness,
Ulverston LA12 0LA. 01229 584280,
www.ulverstonbrewing.co.uk
Offering a range of beers, mostly named after one of Ulverstons famous sons - Stan Laurel.

BEVERAGES

COWMIRE HALL
Cowmire Hall, Crosthwaite, Kendal, Cumbria LA8 8JJ.
01539 568200, www.cowmire.co.uk
Cowmire damsons are skilfully married to London Gin to produce a damson gin which, not being too sweet, can be served as an aperitif and as a liqueur.

CUMBRIAN LEGENDARY ALES
Old Hall Brewery, Hawkshead, Ambleside LA22 0QF.
01539 436436,
www.cumbrianlegendaryales.com
Brewed on the shores of Esthwaite Water, these superb beers are named after famous Cumbrian characters of the past.

HARDKNOT BREWERY
The Woolpack Inn, Boot, Eskdale, Cumbria CA19 1TH.
01946 723230,
www.woolpack.co.uk
Steeped in history, The Woolpack dates from 1578 and serves a fantastic range of beers and ales.

BAKERY

BRYSONS OF KESWICK
42 Main St, Keswick, CA12 5JD. 01768 772257,
www.brysonsofkeswick.co.uk
Baking fresh goods every day, this company produces the widest range of breads, cakes, morning goods and cream cakes.

MORE? THE ARTISAN BAKERY
Mill Yard, Staveley, Kendal LA8 9LR.
www.moreartisan.co.uk
The finest quality, natural ingredients used in breads and patisseries. If you're a 'foodie' or bread connoisseur, try this out!

MOODY BAKER CO-OP
3, West View, Front St, Alston, Cumbria CA9 3SF.
01434 382003.
Bread, cakes, snacks and biscuits all produced using the most natural and local ingredients possible.

THE STAFF OF LIFE
2, Berry's Yard, Kendal LA9 4AB. 01539 738606,
www.artisanbreadmakers.co.uk
Many specialist products made with wheat, rye, barley and oats.

VILLAGE BAKERY
Memerby, Penrith, Cumbria CA10 1HE.
01768 881811,
www.villagebakery.com
A pioneering organic bakery established 30 years ago using natural processes and artisan methods.

CONFECTIONERY

CHOCOLATEHOUSE 1657
57, Branthwaite Brow, Kendal, LA9 4TX. 01539 740702,
www.chocolatehouse1657.co.uk
An Aladdin's cave of chocolates and gifts plus a chocolate restaurant where you can enjoy chocolate drinks, gateaux and ice creams.

KENNEDYS FINE CHOCOLATES
The Old School, Orton, Penrith, Cumbria CA10 3RU.
01539 624 781.
Manufacturers and retailers of fine handmade chocolates.

SAUNDERS CHOCOLATES
Rheged Centre, Redhills, Penrith, Cumbria CA11 0DQ.
01768 860098,
www.saunderschocolates.co.uk
Established in 2003 visitors can view fine chocolates and truffles being made in our kitchen workshop.

TRUFFLES
2, Kingswater close, Brampton, Cumbria
CA8 1PD. 01697 742539, www.truffleschocolates.co.uk
Handmade British gourmet chocolate truffles using only the very finest chocolate, real fruit and local fresh Cumbrian cream.

DAIRY

CHURCHMOUSE CHEESE
Cumberland Dairy, Knock Cross, Longmarton, Appleby,
CA16 6BX. 08453 707020,
www.thecumberlanddairy.co.uk
*Producer of local cheeses Blengdale Blue, Roegill Red,
Cobble Tasty and Keldthwaite Gold.*

HOLKER FARM CHEESE
The Estates Office, Cark-Inn-Cartmel, Cumbria
LA11 7PH. 01539 559084,
www.holkerfoodhall.co.uk
*Award Winning ewes milk cheeses now distributed
across the UK.*

LOW SIZERGH BARN
Sizergh, Kendal, Cumbria LA8 8AE. 01539 560426,
www.lowsizerghbarn.co.uk
*Farmshop, tea room, craft gallery and farm trail. The
farmshop is filled with a huge selection of specialist
Cumbrian foods.*

THE LAKE DISTRICT CHEESE COMPANY
The Lake District Creamery, Aspatria, Wigton CA7 2AR.
01697 320 218, www.lakedistrictcheesecompany.co.uk
*A farmer owned cooperative set in magnificent Cumbrian
countryside producing a range of premium cheeses
crafted with milk from local dairy farms.*

THORNBY MOOR DAIRY
Crofton Hall, Thursby, Carlisle, Cumbria CA5 6QB.
01697 345555.
*Producing a range of cows', goats' and ewes' milk cheeses
using raw milk supplied from single herds within Cumbria.*

FARM SHOPS

COUNTRY CUTS ORGANIC MEATS
Bridge End Farm, Santon Bridge, Holmrook, Cumbria
CA19 1UY, 01946 726256, www.country-cuts.co.uk
*A family run organic farm producing clover fed mature
Aberdeen Angus / Limousin beef, Tender Hill and
Lowland mutton and lamb.*

GREYSTONE HOUSE FARM AND TEAROOM
Greystone House, Stainton, Penrith CA11 0EF.
01768 866 952, www.greystonehousefarm.co.uk
*Award winning farm shop and tea room and producer
of organic beef and lamb.*

HOWBARROW ORGANIC FARM
Cartmel, Grange over Sands, Cumbria LA11 7SS.
01539 536330, www.howbarroworganic.co.uk
*Producers of lamb, beef and seasoned poultry as well as an
extensive range of in season vegetables, salads and herbs.*

KITRIDDING FARM
Lupton, Kirkby Longsdale LA6 2QA.
01539 567484, www.kitridding.co.uk
*Traditionally reared Swaledale lamb, homebred beef and
homemade sausages.*

NATLAND MILLBECK FARM AND ICE CREAM PARLOUR
Natland Millbeck Lane, Kendal LA9 7LH.
01539 729 333, www.millbeckicecream.co.uk
*Delicious ice cream made on the premises and available for
sale in the parlour.*

PLUMGARTHS FOOD PARK AND FARM SHOP
Crook Road, Kendal, Cumbria LA8 8QJ.
01539 736136,
www.plumgarths.co.uk
*Developed by the Geldards, a traditional Cumbrian farming
family, you can purchase a wide variety of natural,
wholesome high quality local food.*

RAYNE COTTAGE
Gaisgill, Penrith, Cumbria CA10 3UD. 01539 624129.
*We breed Gloucester spot pigs, Aberdeen Angus beef and
lamb on our farm near Tebay.*

SILLFIELD FARM
Endmoor, Kendal, Cumbria LA8 0HZ.
01539 567609.
*Produce farm-made food from free range rare breed pigs
and wild boar. As well as home made sausages and salamis,
Westmorland Cheese and a range of naturally smoked
cheeses are available.*

WELLINGTON JERSEYS ICE CREAM AND TEAROOMS
Wellington Farm, Cockermouth, Cumbria CA13 0QU.
01900 822777.
Ice cream is made from the Stamper family's milk from their own herd of pedigree Jersey cattle. Home cooked meals and traybakes are also available.

FISH

BESSY BECK TROUT FISHERY
Greenhead House, Newbiggin on Lune, Kirkby Stephen
CA17 4LY. 01539 623303,
www.bessybecktrout.co.uk
Trout farm and producer of fish terrines and plates. The shop is stocked with fine local produce like venison and herb fed beef and lamb. Cakes, fudge and lots more are also for sale.

FURNESS FISH POULTRY AND GAME SUPPLIES
Moor Lane, Flookburgh, Grange-over-Sands LA11 7LS.
01539 559544, www.morecambebayshrimps.com
Shrimps are caught locally by fishermen using tractors and dragging nets along the sea floor. Coated in butter the shrimps have a flavour of their own. All types of game and a selection of pies are available.

SOLWAY SHELL FISHERIES LTD
Windmill, Black Dyke,
Silloth on Solway CA7 4PZ.
An oyster farm off the Solway Coast.

MEAT

FAR EDGE ORGANIC
Far Branthwaite Edge, Branthwaite,
Workington CA14 4TB. 01900 602428,
www.faredge-organic.com
A family run business selling organic beef and lamb direct to the public and the catering trade.

GREYSTONE HOUSE FARM AND TEAROOM
Greystone House, Stainton, Penrith CA11 0EF.
01768 866 952, www.greystonehousefarm.co.uk
Award winning farm shop and tea room and producer of organic beef and lamb.

HADRIAN ORGANICS
Grainbrow, Hethersgill, Carlisle CA6 6HD.
01228 675252, www.hadrianorganics.co.uk
Organic producers that sell to the public a wide range of quality, organic farm produce naturally reared in north Cumbria.

HERB FED BEEF AND LAMB
Adamthwaite, Ravenstonedale, Kirkby Stephen,
Cumbria CA17 4NW. 01539 623207.
Breeds beef and lamb on protected pastures with rare herbs and flowered in the Howgills.

HOLKER SALT MARSH LAMB
Holker Estates Co Ltd., The Estates Office, Cark-in-
Cartmel, Cumbria LA11 7PH. 01539 558313.
Saltmarsh lamb, reared on Cumbrian Saltmarshes, has long been regarded as a rare delicacy in French Restaurants. Whole and half lamb delivered directly to your door.

KENDAL ROUGH FELL SHEEP MEAT PRODUCERS
High Carlinghill, Tebay, Penrith CA10 3XX.
01539 624 661.
Half and Quarter packs of lamb from Kendal's local breed of sheep are sold here.

KITRIDDING FARM
Lupton, Kirkby Longsdale LA6 2QA. 01539 567484, www.kitridding.co.uk
Traditionally reared Swaledale lamb, homebred beef and homemade sausages.

LOWTHER ORGANIC
Lowther Park Farms, The Estate Office, Lowther, Penrith CA10 2HG. 01931 712407
www.lowtherparkfarms.co.uk
The Lowther family has been producing quality food and organic food on the 3,000 acre estate for nearly 800 years.

Cooked Meat & Pies

BURBUSH PENRITH LTD
The Eden Game Bakery, Gilwilly Road, Gilwilly Industrial Estate, Penrith CA11 9BL. 01768 863841,
www.burbushs.co.uk
Envied with a 20 year history, all their pies are made, finished and packed by hand using locally sourced, quality and traceable ingredients.

RICHARD WOODALL
Lane End, Waberthwaite, Millom LA19 5YJ.
01229 717237, www.richardwoodall.co.uk
The company, currently run by seventh and eighth generation family members, including businessman Richard Woodall, is renowned for its much acclaimed cured hams, bacon and sausages.

SILLFIELD FARM
Endmoor, Kendal, Cumbria LA8 0HZ.
01539 567609.
Produce farm-made food from free range rare breed pigs and wild boar. As well as home made sausages and salamis, Westmorland Cheese and a range of naturally smoked cheeses are available.

THE PIE MILL
Unit 16, Blencathra Business Centre, Threlkeld, Keswick CA12 4TR. 01768 779994, www.piemill.co.uk
Tried and tested pies at The Mill Inn for years, this superb range of quality homemade pies has only the best local ingredients.

Preserves, Relishes, Honey & Puddings

BORDER COUNTY FOODS
Kingmoor Barn, Kingmoor Park, Carlisle CA6 4SP.
01228 672020.
North West fine food producer of the year, 2004, is famous for their Cumberland sausages made from rare breed pork.

CONISTON COUNTRY KITCHEN LARDER
Coniston Lodge, Coniston, Cumbria LA21 8HH.
01539 441201, www.coniston-lodge.com
Award winning handmade produce. Chutneys, jams, marmalade and Coniston Lodge gingerbread. Beautiful hampers available.

COUNTRY FLAVOUR
15 High Street, Kirkby Stephen, Cumbria CA17 4SG.
01768 371124, www.country-flavour.co.uk
Family business since 1948. Homemade products include fudge, toffee, lemon cheese, marmalade, herb jellies, jam from local fruit and brandy butter.

CUMBERLAND MUSTARD
16 Hillhouse Lane, Alston, Cumbria CA9 3TN.
01434 381135, www.cumberlandmustard.com
Fully traceable high quality goods; unique honey mustards and a range of pickles and vinaigrettes using our special raspberry vinegar.

DEMELS
Cross Lane, Ulverston, Cumbria LA12 9DQ.
01434 381135, www.demels.co.uk
*Tantalising award winning chutneys and pickle, handmade
to traditional Sri Lankan recipes. Excellent marinade and
a treat with curries.*

HAWKSHEAD RELISH CO LTD
The Square, Hawkshead, Ambleside LA22 0NZ.
01539 436614, www.hawksheadrelish.com
*Over 100 award winning relishes are handmade ranging
from pickles and preserves, mustards, sauces flavoured oils
and vinegars. The shop is open every day in Hawkshead
and available online.*

LIZZIE'S HOME MADE
The Bank, Dockray. Penrith CA11 0LG. 01768 482487,
www.fruttacotta.co.uk
*A delicious pudding of figs, apricots and prunes in
Cumbrian spiced rum syrup.*

NOOK FARM HONEY
Nook Farm, Bailey, Cumbria TD9 0TR. 01697 748317,
www.nookfarmhoney.co.uk
*Specialty wildflower honey, borage honey and balsam
honey from the Nook Farm Bees forage.*

WILD AND FRUITFUL
Hillside, Cuddy Lonning, Wigton, Cumbria CA7 0AA.
01697 344304.
*Handmade jams, jellies, oils and vinegars in unusual
combinations as well as old favourites. Jars are
labelled with the origin of ingredients (even down to
a specific tree!).*

PUDDING ROOM
Old Browne Howe Barn, Water Yeat, Coniston,
Cumbria LA12 8DW. 01229 885670.
*Our puddings include the best quality Belgian chocolate
to be enjoyed by connoisseurs of fine dining.*

SARAH NELSON'S GRASMERE GINGERBREAD SHOP
Church Cottage, Grasmere, Ambleside,
Cumbria LA22 9SW. 01539 435428,
www.grasmeregingerbread.co.uk
*Although world famous it can only be purchased in the
shop in Grasmere or by mail order. Awarded Gold Award
for traditional rum butter. Also stock other
Cumbrian products.*

SWEET HOME
Briardale, Millans Park, Ambleside,
Cumbria LA22 9AG. 01539 434070.
*Delicious handmade puddings, boasting a big time fan
base of those "in the know", now available commercially.*

ULTIMATE PLUM PUDDING CO LTD
Units 9-10, Beezan Rd Trading Est., Kendal, LA9 6BW.
01539 734144, www.ultimateplumpudding.co.uk
*Infinitely flexible, our light and delicious luxury Christmas
pudding is available in gold packaging or it can be
personalised for a retail private label, fundraising or gifts.*

Smoked Foods

BORDER COUNTY FOODS
Kingmoor Barn, Kingmoor Park, Carlisle CA6 4SP.
01228 672020.
*North West fine food producer of the year, 2004, is famous
for their Cumberland sausages made from rare breed pork.*

LAKELAND BARN ARTISAN FOODS
Howestone Barn, Whinfell, Kendall, Cumbria LA8 9EQ.
01539 824373.
*Produce from traditional breeds slowly reared outdoors in
Cumbria include, dry-cure bacon, traditional prime meat
sausage and continental style charcuterie.*

OLD SMOKE HOUSE AND TRUFFLES CHOCOLATES
Brougham Hall, Brougham, Penrith, Cumbria CA10 2DE.
01768 867772, www.the-old-smokehouse.co.uk
*We have won over 14 great taste awards since 2002,
including several for our duck breast. Each local produce is
individually smoked over oak and has a wonderful flavour.*

RICHARD WOODALL
Lane End, Waberthwaite, Millom LA19 5YJ.
01229 717237, www.richardwoodall.co.uk
*The company, currently run by seventh and eighth
generation family members, including businessman Richard
Woodall, is renowned for its much acclaimed cured hams,
bacon and sausages.*

SADDLEBACK FOODS AND SMOKERIE
Scarfoot, Plumpton, Penrith, Cumbria CA11 9PF.
01768 885599, www.saddlebackfoods.co.uk
*Our family farm offers fresh meat and poultry alongside our
existing range of smoked produce, patés and ready meals.*

204 CONTRIBUTORS

BORROWDALE GATES HOTEL
Grange in Borrowdale, Keswick, Cumbria CA12 5UQ
01768 777 204
www.borrowdale-gates.com

THE BROWN HORSE INN
Winster, Cumbria LA23 3NR
01539 443 443
www.thebrownhorseinn.co.uk

CRAGWOOD COUNTRY HOUSE HOTEL
Ecclerigg, Windermere, Cumbria LA23 1LQ
01539 488 177
www.cragwoodhotel.co.uk

DALE LODGE HOTEL
Red Bank Road, Grasmere,
Cumbria LA22 9SW
015394 35300
www.dalelodgehotel.co.uk

FAYRER GARDEN HOUSE HOTEL
Lyth Valley Road, Bowness on Windermere, Cumbria LA23 3JP
015394 88195
www.fayrergarden.com

GILPIN LODGE HOTEL
Crook Road, Windermere, Cumbria LA23 3NE
01539 488 818
www.gilpinlodge.co.uk

THE GLASS HOUSE RESTAURANT
Rydal Road, Ambleside, Cumbria LA22 9AN
01539 432 137
www.theglasshouserestaurant.co.uk

JERICHOS
College Road, Windermere, Cumbria LA23 1BX
01539 442 522
www.jerichos.co.uk

PURDEYS RESTAURANT
The Langdale Estate, Great Langdale, Near Ambleside,
Cumbria LA22 9JD
01539 438 080
www.langdale.co.uk

MEREWOOD COUNTRY HOUSE HOTEL
Ecclerigg, Windermere, Cumbria LA23 1LH
01539 446 484
www.merewoodhotel.co.uk

MILLER HOWE RESTAURANT AND HOTEL
Rayrigg Road, Windermere, Cumbria LA23 1EY
01539 442 536
www.millerhowe.com

THE QUINCE AND MEDLAR
13 Castlegate, Cockermouth, Cumbria CA13 9EU
01900 823 579
www.quinceandmedlar.co.uk

RAMPSBECK COUNTRY HOUSE HOTEL
Watermillock, Ullswater, Cumbria CA11 0LP
01768 486 442
www.rampsbeck.co.uk

ROTHAY MANOR HOTEL
Ambleside, Cumbria
LA22 0EH
01539 433 605
www.rothaymanor.co.uk

THE SAMLING
Ambleside Road, Windermere, Cumbria LA23 1LR
01539 431 922
www.thesamlinghotel.co.uk

SHARROW BAY COUNTRY HOUSE HOTEL
Lake Ullswater, Penrith, Cumbria
CA10 2LZ
01768 486 301
www.sharrowbay.co.uk

THE SUN INN
6 Market Street, Kirkby Lonsdale, Cumbria LA6 2AU
01524 271 965
www.sun-inn.info

THE SWAN HOTEL AND SPA
Newby Bridge, Cumbria LA12 8NB
01539 531 681
www.swanhotel.com

WINDER HALL COUNTRY HOUSE HOTEL
Low Lorton, Cockermouth, Cumbria CA13 9UP
0190 085 107
www.winderhall.co.uk

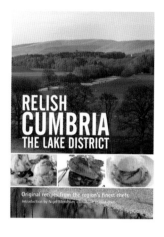

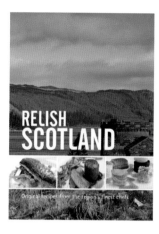

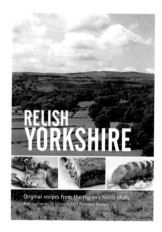

Good food is all about passion, creativity, taste and experience. But it takes the talents of enthusiastic and truly innovative chefs to bring it to our attention – and make us want more.

Relish Cumbria champions the very best restaurants in this beautiful county, who offer their own unique take on the freshest and best local ingredients in recipes for you to create and try at home.

There is much to celebrate. From fresh line caught Sea Bass, local Herdwick lamb, not to mention an abundance of fresh vegetables, dairy produce and artisan gourmet products.

The magic ingredient, of course, is the talent of chefs from this selection of fine-dining restaurants and country house hotels.

All the chefs featured here have given away the secrets of some of their signature dishes just for you, so go on, create something delicious today.

For more information on other books in this series and to receive and share recipes online please visit, www.relishpublications.co.uk

RELISH
PUBLICATIONS.CO.UK